Education For The 21st Century

EDUCATION FOR THE 21st CENTURY

Editor
Dr. Digumarti Bhaskara Rao
M.Sc., M.A., M.A., M.Ed., Ph.D.
R.V.R. College of Education
D-43, Srinivasa Nagar Colony
Guntur - 522 006
Andhra Pradesh
India

DISCOVERY PUBLISHING HOUSE
NEW DELHI

First Published - 2001

Reprinted - 2017

ISBN: 978-81-7141-389-8

Education for the 21st Century

Published by:

DISCOVERY PUBLISHING HOUSE PVT. LTD.

4383/4B, Ansari Road, Darya Ganj
New Delhi-110 002 (India)
Phone: +91-11-23279245, 43596064-65
Fax: +91-11-23253475
E-mail: discoverypublishinghouse@gmail.com
sales@discoverypublishinggroup.com
web: www.discoverypublishinggroup.com

Printed at:
Infinity Imaging Systems
Delhi

PREFACE

The twenty-first century, due to globalisation, will bring forth many more successes, achievements, luxuries, facilities, innovations, inventions opportunities, advancements and developments along with various types of tensions, frustrations, conflicts, restrictions, oppressions, violations, violences, troubles and even wars; and hence there will be a challenge of reinventing the democratic ideals to create social cohesion. Education in this context has to play a pivotal role in reducing tensions, conflicts, poverty, ignorance, oppression and war.

New approaches are required in education to make learning to live, learning to lead, and learning to develop. Universal basic education must be made a priority. Secondary education must show ways and means for the development of integrated societies. Higher education must be the centre of knowledge to show light to the mankind.

As the International Commission on Education for the Twenty-first Century, under the Chairmanship of the former European Commission President Mr. Jacques Delors proposed in its report — Learning : The Treasure Within — to UNESCO, that the four pillars of education should be learning to be, learning to know, learning to do, and learning to live together.

The papers, which are presented in this book, prepared to , for and about the International Commission on Education for the Twenty-first Century are very much critical, analytical informative, valuable and resourceful. The readers of this book can enlighten themselves about the education to be advocated in the twenty-first century. This book will show a way, in its little sense, to educationists in designing education for the twenty-first century.

D. Bhaskara Rao

ACKNOWLEDGEMENTS

I

am thankful to

Mr. Federico Mayor

Mr. Jacques Delors

Mr. Asher Deleon

Ms. Alexandra Draxler

Ms. Fay Chung

Mr. R. Diez-Hochleitner

UNESCO

UNICEF

International Commission on Education
for the 21st Century

International Consultative Forum on EFA

The UNESCO Courier

UNESCO Sources

and authors

whose contributions and cooperation

made this publication possible

for making the education

a success story in the 21st Century

D. B. RAO

CONTENTS

1

Education for Tomorrow

— Jacques Delors

[In 1993, UNESCO set up an independent International Commission on Education for the 21st century, chaired by Mr. Jacques Delors. The Commission, whose members and advisors were drawn from the major world regions, has completed its work after a worldwide process of consultation and analysis over a period of three years. Mr. Delors presents a roundup of the main issues studied by the Commission and previews some of its conclusions.]

On the eve of the twenty first century, intense thought and discussion are being devoted to the future of human society. Whereas advances in knowledge, especially in science and technology, bring hope of progress for humankind in the future, events each day remind us how the contemporary world is liable to drift off course, how exposed it is to dangers, in some cases extreme dangers, and how vulnerable it is to conflicts.

The increasing interdependence of peoples and nations, which is the hallmark of our time, is providing scope for unprecedented international co-operation. But the emergence of this global consciousness also reveals the extent of the disparities that beset our world, the complexity of its problems and the number of threats that are liable at any time to jeopardize the stock of human achievement.

Great demands are consequently being made on

education, whose contribution to human progress is so vital. The idea is gaining ground that education is one of the most powerful tools with which to shape the future—or, to use more modest terms, to steer us into the future by taking advantage of constructive trends and trying to avoid pitfalls. What is education doing today to prepare the active citizens of tomorrow?

UNESCO has taken the initiative of bringing the light of its international experience to bear on the issue. Its Director-General, Mr. Federico Mayor, asked me to chair an International Commission on Education for the Twenty-first Century, mandated "to study and reflect on the challenges facing education in the coming years, and to formulate suggestions and recommendations in the form of a report that could serve as an agenda for action for policy makers and officials at the highest levels."

The following question from the Commission's terms and reference formed our point of departure : "How can education play a dynamic and constructive role in preparing individuals and societies for the twenty-first century?" We were asking it some twenty years after another Commission, chaired by Mr. Edgar Faure, had published a report which is still topical—under the significant title *Learning to Be.*

Four Crucial Issues

The Commission did its best to project its thinking on to a future dominated by globalization, to ask the right questions and to lay down some broad guidelines that can be applied both within national contexts and on a global scale. Here I shall examine four issues which I believe are crucial.

The first issue is the capacity of education systems to become the key factor in development by performing a threefold function—economic, scientific and cultural. Everyone expects education to help build up a qualified and creative workforce that can adapt to new technologies and take part in the "intelligence revolution" that is the driving force of our economies. Everyone—in North and South alike—also expects education to advance knowledge in such a way that economic development goes hand in hand with responsible management of the physical and human environment. And, finally education would be failing in its task if it did not produce citizens rooted in their own cultures and yet open to other cultures and committed to the progress of society.

The second crucial issue is the ability of education systems to adapt to new trends in society. This brings us to one of the fundamental responsibilities of education—having to prepare for change despite the growing insecurity that fills us with doubts and uncertainties. Education must take into account a whole range of interrelated and interacting factors that are always in a state of flux, whether it is dealing with individual or social values, family structure, the role of women, the status accorded to minorities, or the problems of urban development or the environment.

The third crucial issue is that of the relations between the education system and the state. The roles and responsibilities of the state, the devolution of some of its powers to federal or local authorities, the balance to be struck between public and private education—these are just some aspects of a problem which, moreover, differs from one country to another.

The fourth issue is the promulgation of the values of openness to others, and mutual understanding—in a word, the values of peace. Can education purport to be universal? Can it by itself, as a historical factor, create a universal language that would make it possible to overcome certain contradictions, respond to certain challenges and, despite their diversity, convey a message to all the inhabitants of the world? In this language which, ideally, would be accessible to everybody, all the world's wisdom and the wealth of its civilizations and cultures would be expressed in an immediately comprehensible form.

The creation of a language accessible to everyone would mean that people would learn to engage more readily in dialogue, and the message that this language would convey would have to be addressed to human beings in all their aspects. A message that claims to be universal—one of education's lofty ambitions—must be conveyed with all the subtle qualifications that take full account of human beings' infinite variety. This is no doubt our major difficulty.

Lines of Enquiry

Three current crises—the economic crisis, the crisis of the ideology of progress and a certain form of moral crisis—formed the backdrop to the Commission's work.

With them in mind, I tried to trace out a few lines of enquiry, taking account of cultural diversity, the specific nature of different problems and experiences, and the diversity of the political and social objectives of UNESCO's Member States, so as to gain a better understanding of a number of fundamental relationships : the connection between education and culture (culture being seen as a factor in greater self-knowledge and knowledge of others); between education and citizenship and, more generally, the sense of belonging (so that our contemporaries and descendants do not feel isolated in the world of exceptionally rapid change which they see on their television screens); between education and social cohesion (which is weaker than it was fifty years ago in the countries of both North and South). And then, of course, the connection between education, training, work and employment; the connection with development; and lastly, the essential role which education must play in the progress of research.

If the proposals that emerged from the Commission's work were to have a real impact on education policies, three transversal problems also had to be tackled. These were: the effect of modern communication media on contemporary education systems; the future of the teaching profession; the systems to be set up and the funding to be found.

The Pillars of Education

The four main pillars that the Commission has presented and illustrated as the bases of education are : learning to know, learning to do, learning to be and learning to live together.

The first of these is learning to know. Bearing in mind the rapid changes brought about the scientific progress and new forms of economic and social activity, there is a need to combine a broad general education with the possibility of working in depth on a selected number of subjects. In a sense, such a general education is the passport to learning throughout life, insofar as it should teach people to enjoy learning and also lay the foundations that will enable them to carry on learning throughout their lives.

Learning to do is the second pillar. In addition to learning to practise a profession or trade, people need to develop the ability to face a variety of situations and to work in teams, a feature of educational methods that does not receive enough attention at present. These skills are more readily acquired if pupils and students have the opportunity to develop their abilities by becoming involved in work experience schemes or social work while they are still in education. Increased importance should thus be attached to all schemes in which education alternates with work.

Learning to be was the theme of the Edgar Faure Report published under UNESCO's auspices in 1972. The Report's recommendations are still extremely relevant, for in the twenty first century everyone will need to exercise greater independence and judgement combined with a stronger sense of personal responsibility for the attainment of common goals. Learning to live together, finally, by developing an understanding of others, of their history, their traditions and their spirituality. This would provide a basis for the creation of a new spirit which, guided by recognition of our growing interdependence and a common analysis of the risks and challenges of the future, would induce people to implement common projects or to manage the inevitable conflicts in an intelligent and peaceful way. Some might say that this is utopian; and yet it is a necessary utopia, indeed a vital one if we are to escape from the dangerous cycle sustained by cynicism and complacency.

Learning Throughout Life

The concept of learning throughout life advocated in the Faure Report is one of the keys to the twenty-first century. It meets the challenge of a rapidly changing world, and it is necessary because of its advantages of flexibility, diversity and availability at different times and in different places. It also goes beyond the traditional distinction between initial schooling and continuing education.

The idea of lifelong education must be rethought and broadened. As well as adapting to changes in working life, it should also comprise a continuous shaping of the personality, of knowledge and aptitudes, but also the critical faculty and the ability to act.

The truth is that every aspect of working life and social life offers opportunities for both learning and doing. There is a great temptation to make too much of this, and stress the educational potential of the media, the world of work, and cultural and leisure pursuits, even to the extent of forgetting a number of fundamental truths. Although people need to use all these opportunities for learning and self improvement, they will not be able to make good use of all their potential unless they have received a sound basic education. School should impart a desire for and pleasure in learning, the ability to learn how to learn, and intellectual curiosity. One might even imagine a society in which each individual would be in turn both teacher and learner.

The basis for a learning society is a formal system where each individual is introduced to the many different forms of knowledge. There is no substitute for the teacher-pupil relationship based on authority and dialogue. This has been said time and again by the great classical thinkers who have studied the question of education. It is the teacher's responsibility to impart to the pupil the knowledge that humankind has acquired about itself and about nature, and the essence of human creativity and inventiveness.

Education should therefore constantly be adapting to changes in society, and also pass on the attainments, foundations and benefits of human experience.

The Stages and Bridges of Learning : A Fresh Approach

By focusing on the concept of learning throughout life, the Commission did not intend to convey the idea that one could avoid reflecting on the different levels of education. The fact is that learning throughout life makes it possible to reorder the sequences and itineraries of education, ease the transition from one stage to another and recognize the value of each.

The "three Rs"—reading, writing and arithmetic—get their full due. The combination of conventional teaching and out-of-school approaches should enable children to experience the three dimensions of education—the moral and cultural, the scientific and technological, and economic and social.

Basic education should be provided worldwide for 900 million illiterate adults, 130 million children not enrolled in school, and more than 100 million who drop out prematurely. This vast undertaking is a priority for technical assistance and partnership carried out through international co-operation.

One major problem area in any reform concerns the policies to be adopted for young people after primary education. One might go so far as to say that secondary schools tend to be neglected in educational thinking. They are the target of considerable criticism and provoke a considerable amount of frustration.

One source of frustration is a demand for expansion and diversification of secondary education, leading to rapid growth in enrolments and congestion in teaching programmes. This gives rise to some classic problems of mass education which developing countries cannot easily solve either financially or in terms of organization. Furthermore, there is the discouraging problem of school leavers who face a shortage of opportunities, their distress increased by a widespread all-or-nothing obsession with access to higher education. Mass unemployment in many countries has exacerbated this maláise.

The only way out of this difficult situation seems to be a very broad diversification of types of study available. The latter should include both conventional education, which focuses more on abstraction and conceptualization, and approaches that combine school and job experience in a way that brings out other abilities and inclinations. In any event, there should be bridges between these approaches so that errors in choice of direction, which are far too widespread, can be corrected.

Furthermore, the prospect of being able to go back to education or training would alter the general climate by assuring each young person that his or her fate is not sealed between the ages of fourteen and twenty.

Higher education should be seen from the same angle.

In many countries, other types of higher education institutions exist side by side with universities. Some are highly selective, while others were set up to provide specifically targeted, quality professional and vocational training. This diversification obviously meets the needs of society and the economy, both at the national and regional levels.

Increasingly stringent selection in order to ease the pressures brought about by mass higher education in the wealthiest countries is neither politically nor socially acceptable. One of the main flaws in such an approach is that many young people are expelled from the educational process before they have been able to obtain a recognized diploma and find themselves in the desperate predicament of having neither a degree nor training appropriate for the job market.

There is a need to manage increasing university enrolment in tandem with reform of secondary education.

Universities would contribute to this process by diversifying what they offers as scientific establishments and centres of learning leading to theoretical or applied research or teaching; as establishments offering professional qualifications, with courses and content tailored to the needs of the economy; as one of the main crossroads for learning throughout life; as leading partners in a form of international co-operation favoring exchanges of teachers and students and promoting the wider availability of first class teaching through international professorships.

These proposals have a special significance in poor countries, where universities have a decisive role to play.

Long-term Strategies for Reform

Without underestimating the obligation to manage short-term constraints or disregard the need to adapt existing systems, the Commission emphasized the need for a longer-term approach if necessary reforms are to succeed. By the same token, it stressed the fact that reforms introduced in rapid succession cancel each other out, since they do not allow the system the time needed either to absorb change or to involve all those concerned in the process.

Three main protagonists contribute to the success of educational reforms; the local community (parents, school heads and teachers), the public authority and the international community.

Local community participation in assessing needs by means of a dialogue between the public authorities and social groups concerned is a first essential stage in broadening access to education and improving its quality. Continuing the dialogue by way of the media, community discussions, parent education and training, and on-the-job teacher training usually arouses greater awareness, develops judgment and helps build local capacities.

In any event, no reform can succeed without the co-operative and active participation of teachers. The Commission recommended that the social, cultural and material status of educators should be considered as a matter of priority, along with the tools required to deliver education of a high standard: books, modern communication media, and suitable cultural and economic support for the school.

This being so, one requirement for the improvement of education systems is responsible public policy. Policy makers cannot assume that the market can compensate for the failures in the system or that laisser-faire is sufficient. The public authorities must propose clear options and, after broad consultation with all concerned, choose policies that set guidelines for the system and lay its foundations, and regulate it by making the necessary adjustments.

All the choices to be made should be predicated upon the principle of equal opportunity.

During the Commission's deliberations, I put forward proposal that may be regarded as radical. As education throughout life gradually becomes a reality, all young persons could be allocated an education voucher at the start of their education. This would entitle them to a certain number of years of education. Their entitlement would be credited to an account at a bank which would manage a capital of time available for each individual, together with the appropriate funds. Everyone could use their capital for schooling, on the basis of their own choices. Some of the capital could be set aside to enable people to receive continuing education during their adult lives. Each person could increase his or her capital through deposits at the bank under a kind of educational savings scheme.

The Commission supported this idea, though it was aware of potential deviations that might prejudice equality of opportunity, and considered that vouchers might be allocated not at the beginning but at the end of compulsory schooling so as to enable adolescents to choose a path without jeopardizing their future choices.

As far as the international community is concerned, as agent of the success of educational reforms, the Commission framed a number of suggestions concerning: a policy of strong encouragement for the education of girls and women; the allocation of a minimum percentage of development aid (a quarter of the total) to fund education; the development of debt-for-education swaps to offset the adverse effects on state education expenditure of adjustment policies and policies for reducing internal and external deficits; the widespread introduction of the new technologies of the "information society" in all countries, to prevent the growth of yet another gap between rich countries and poor countries; enlisting the outstanding potential of non-governmental organizations.

These few suggestions should be seen in the context of partnership rather than aid. After so many failures and so much waste, experience militates in favour of partnership. Globalization makes it inescapable.

Conclusion

The interdependence of nations provides scope for—and requires—international cooperation on a new scale and in all fields. The International Commission on Education for the Twenty-first Century is one of the ways of asserting the will to achieve this as the turn of the century draws near.

Without conducting a purely descriptive exercise or outlining a philosophy of education systems, its goal was not to construct "scenarios for the future" resulting in a set of precepts for educational policy-makers, but to provide decision-makers with facts to help them draw up educational policies and to spark off a debate that would go beyond the world of education and teachers, and involve parents, children, business leaders, trade unionists and associations engaged in giving education a more effective role.

(Source : The UNESCO Courier, April 1996)

2

Education for the 21st Century : A Lifetime to Learn

— *Ricardo Diez-Hochleitner*

Learning to know, learning to do, learning to live together and learning to be: these four pillars should be the foundations for any educational vision in the 21st century. Going one step further, the Delors Report sees them as the basis for a society valorizing lifelong learning at the heart of society, a concept our dossier illustrates through a generation by generation approach, starting with an actor in his golden sixties who shares his musical wisdom with children. In the US, a preschool programme teaches tolerance at an early age, while in Egypt, community schools in remote areas adopt a student-centred strategy. Lifelong education provides opportunities, as in Jamaica, where teenagers learn the ropes of the hotel trade. It's also about second chances: in Thailand, companies share their know-how with villagers while in eastern Germany, technical training centres help women enter the market economy. Still, despite government pledges recognizing its promise, especially in the context of globalization and rapid technological change, lifelong education remains far from a reality.

The publication of the *Report of the International Commission on Education for the Twenty First Century*, sponsored by UNESCO, is perfectly timed. The century that is drawing to a close has been one of immense paradoxes, with its share of horrors, achievements and unfulfilled hopes. It has been marked by two world wars, horrendous genocides, rapid degradation of the biosphere and the exclusion of rising numbers from the increasing prosperity of the rich. But it has also been a century of great progress in science and technology, which has been marked by the Universal Declaration of Human Rights.

Today, with all the knowledge available to us, we have plenty of reasons for optimism, as long as we work together to make sure they bear fruit. For this, we must deepen and extend our knowledge but also live according to ethical and moral values, starting with solidarity and tolerance. This has always been the deep-rooted conviction of educators and of all those who have tried and are trying to do their best for peace and the well-being of peoples; it is also the driving force behind the Report.

Education has always been recognized, though with varying degrees of conviction, as a vital element for individual self fulfilment and the development of society. The 1960s, however, were a particularly propitious decade for investment in education. At that time, the building up of human capital was seen as a key to economic development. The corresponding social development, spurred on by democratization and equality of opportunity, and relatively steady economic growth, created a rising demand for educational services at all levels.

Reacting to Change

Innumerable local and international initiatives and actions were taken to meet this demand. There have been great achievements, though progress has been spasmodic given the presence of many urgent and serious problems. The need to react to changing situations sometimes prevented leaders from seeing that absolute priority should be given to the sustained effort to promote education and training, research and specialized course and to make them available to all those with the talent, ability and perseverance to take advantage of such opportunities.

Although not sufficiently recognized in the Report, the last few decades have quite often offered examples of a massive expansion of forms and levels of education, of educational planning to promote democratization and equity, of comprehensive and ambitious reforms to improve quality and of the principle of lifelong education based on the type of society desired for the near future. These efforts have been made despite the uneven and irregular allocation of resources and the varying degrees of importance attached to the many highly complex aspects linked to the tightly interrelated world of learning and education.

Again and again, what has been missing above all — and this is also the view expressed in the Report - has been a broad vision, clearly defined priorities, realistic strategies for carrying out plans, sufficient independence for educational establishments to attain high overall quality, adequate financial and material resources, sensible use of new technologies and a positive and responsible attitude to creativity and innovation. Nor has there been the common sense needed to take into account cultural identity, legitimate aspirations and each society's concept of unity and progress within the framework of effective international cooperation.

As I see it, the reason why so many limitations and difficulties keep recurring has been the absence of sustained political, social and economic awareness among opinion leaders and the public at large - of the decisive contribution education can make to the resolution of pressing world problems, and to the attainment of more ambitious medium-term national goals, by applying practical methods and procedures suited to each particular case. This would require an intelligent, realistic, ongoing public debate to which all the parties concerned (parents, students, educators, administration, industry, religious and political leaders, trade unionists, etc.) would contribute. Serious debate of this kind would avoid point-scoring and offer solutions geared to changing circumstances, providing regular and objective quantitative and qualitative assessments that would enable improvements and changes to be fed back into the system. This requires a coherent frame of reference, as was the case, for example, in Spain, when a white paper on the overall restructuring of education led to a reform in 1969 designed to achieve lifelong education. Above all, this was the approach of the 1972 report entitled "Learning to be", of the UNESCO Commission chaired by Edgar Faure, which served as a basis for reforms in several countries.

However, at that time the focus was more limited and more affected by events such as the student revolt, which took a clearly political stance, in a society that unimaginatively saw itself as developing in a straight line towards the future.

The challenges of today are much broader. We are no doubt witnessing the rise of a new era, a new civilization work is becoming a person's most precious asset; communications (multimedia and cyberspace) are making massive amounts of information available to everyone, and despite globalization, conflict within local culture is on the rise.

Faced with these challenges, the Report rightly calls for enormous tasks in preparing for the twenty-first century, involving the definition and adoption of new concepts for development and progress (that are at once morally acceptable, effective and viable). It also calls on the political, business and cultural worlds to introduce in each society models of development that are sustainable and appropriate to each situation. We need a type of education that will make an effective contribution to democratic coexistence, tolerance, solidarity and cooperation, in a context of rapid and far reaching change and growing interdependence among different countries, as the Club of Rome has repeatedly pointed out.

The difficult task is further complicated by the fact

that although the education system has helped to effect a break with the past - it has been a decisive ally in support of major social change, economic development and progress in science and technology — it has not completely freed itself from its own past, not even in cases where broad and successful reforms have been carried out. Education is still living in the past because its present social context is totally different from the situation for which it was designed. Education must not only be adapted to the needs of our age, it must also make a real effort to look ahead some 25 years so as to have a vision of a future society that is both desirable and possible to construct.

We are at a crossroads, and it is clear, as the Report points out, that the education and learning system chosen in each country must depend essentially on the kind of society that the people want for themselves and their children. Similarly, the training and apprenticeships of future students in this revitalized lifelong education must take into account the particular rights and responsibilities which they have to accept and assume.

The Will to Mobilize

In claiming our rights, we can and must take the future into our own hands. This starts with carrying out our responsibilities. To this end, we need a basic knowledge and a more specific understanding of our specialized fields. To be a real human being and live in peace, freedom and progress, we need education, namely, a process of learning, training and professionalization backed up by the acquisition of positive habits and attitudes. To achieve this, the society in which we live (beginning with family, business, governments, and cultural, scientific and educational institutions) must be convinced of the need for a collective effort to ensure that each and every one of us is able to turn the dream, hope, right and opportunity into a reality.

Only an open and continuous debate can create the political will to mobilize the necessary human and material resources for a knowledgeable society and to treat human capital as our planet's most important resource. This vital debate, this universal human revolution, can and should be set in motion by the *Report on Education for the Twenty First Century*. It is a model of comprehensiveness, detailed analysis and rigorous synthesis, farsightedness and humanisms. All of which is infused with deep sensitivity and respect for the great diversity of circumstances and cultures.

Ricardo DIEZ-HOCHLEITNER
President, Club of Rome

(Source : UNESCO Courier, April 1996)

3

International Commission on Education for the Twenty-first Century

Preliminary Synthesis

Preamble

On the eve of the twenty-first century, intense thought and discussion is being devoted to the future of human society. Education, on which human progress depends to such a large extent, has not escaped scrutiny. What is it doing today to prepare the active citizens of tomorrow?

It is in this context, and in keeping with the mission of UNESCO, that in November 1991 the General Conference invited the Director Generel to convene an international commission to reflect on education and learning for the twenty-first century. Federico Mayor requested Jacques Delors to chair the Commission, with a group of 14 other persons from all over the world and from varied cultural and professional backgrounds.

The International Commission on Education for the Twenty-First Century was formally established at the beginning of 1993, with a wide-ranging mandate 'to study and reflect on the challenges facing education in the coming years and to formulate suggestions and recommendations in the form of a report that (could) serve as an agenda for renewal and action for policy-makers and official at the highest levels.' Financed by UNESCO and working with the assistance of a secretariat provided by the Organization, the Commission was able to draw on the Organization's valuable resources and international experience and on an impressive mass of information, but was completely independent in carrying out its work and preparing its recommendations.

UNESCO has on several previous occasions produced international studies reviewing issues and priorities in education worldwide. In 1968, *The World Educational Crisis, A Systems Analysis*, by Philip H. Coombs, Director of UNESCO's International Institute for Educational Planning (IIEP), drew on the work of the institute to examine the problems facing education, and to recommend far reaching innovations.

In 1971, in the wake of student upheavals in much of the world during the previous three years, Rene Maheu (then Director-General of UNESCO), asked a former Prime Minister and Minister of Education of France, Edgar Faure, to chair a panel of seven persons entrusted with defining 'the new aims to be assigned to education as a result of the rapid changes in knowledge and in societies, the demands of development, the aspirations of the individual, and the overriding need for international understanding and peace' and putting forward 'suggestions regarding the intellectual, human and financial means needed to attain the objective set....' Published in 1972 under the title **Learning to be**, the report of the Edgar Faure Commission had the great merit of firmly establishing the concept of lifelong learning, at a time when traditional education systems were being challenged.

***

The first and certainly the chief difficulty confronting the Commission in carrying out its mandate concerned the vast diversity of educational situations, philosophies of education and indeed practicalities of educational provision and organization. Related to the difficulties raised by diversity was the sheer quantity of information available, and the impossibility for the Commission of digesting more than a small proportion of it in the course of its work. Thus, selection was necessary to determine what was vital in looking at the future, bearing in mind both geopolitical, economic, social and cultural trends, and potential roles of education policies.

Realizing of course that no choice could please everyone, and on the basis of documentation assembled at both national and international levels, we decided to concentrate on a central theme that could be relevance all over the world, namely, the way in which education can cultivate the creative potential of each individual, and at the same time contribute to promoting cohesion in an increasingly globalized society. Admittedly, everyday reality varies radically from one continent and one country to another. But over and above such diversity, which should never be overlooked, there remains a general view of the importance of education.

Much has been written about how learning takes place, and what circumstances favour different kinds of learning; a great deal is also known about the consequences, for individuals and society, of decisions concerning the organization of school and higher education systems. There is abundant research and evidence concerning the content of formal and non-formal education; and indicators are available, even if inadequate, to evaluate the policies followed. However, the Commission observed early on that effective choice, both individual and societal, are often based on principles that should be examined and taken into account in any study of this kind. It is therefore not surprising that the Commission decided to explain its approach by referring to certain principles, in particular, those underlying the basic objectives of education policy.

***

The method adopted by the Commission was to engage in as wide-ranging a process of consultation as was possible during the time available. The Commission met in plenary session eight times, it held eight working group sessions to examine both the major topic chosen, and also concerns and issues particular to one region or group of countries. Participants in the working group sessions were representative of a wide range of professions and organizations directly and indirectly related to education, formal and non-formal: teachers, researchers, students, government officials, and people active in governmental and non-governmental organizations at national and international levels. Individual hearings of well-known intellectuals enabled the Commission to hold-in-depth exchanges on a wide rage of topics related to education. Other consultations were held on an individual basis, face-to-face or in writing. A questionnaire was sent to all National Commission of UNESCO to invite submissions in the form of existing documentation or fresh material: the response was very positive, and the replies were studied carefully. Non-governmental organizations were similarly consulted and in some cases invited to participate in meetings. In the past two and a half years, members of the Commission, including its Chairman, also attended a series of governmental and non-governmental meetings in which its work was discussed and ideas exchanged.

Many written submissions were requested by, or sent spontaneously to, the Commission. The Commission secretariat analysed a considerable volume of literature and provided summaries on a variety of topics for the commissioners. The Commission will propose that in addition to its report, UNESCO should also publish the working documents produced for it.

Financed by UNESCO and working with the assistance of a secretariat provided by the Organization, the Commission was able to draw on the Organization's valuable resources and international experience and on an impressive mass of information, but was completely independent in carrying out its work and in preparing its recommendations.

On these bases the Commission prepared for the General Conference a concise text summarizing the main analyses and recommendations in the final report.

This text which follows seeks to relate changing trends in the world and societies to the mission, traditionally devolving on education.

***

In the first part of its report the Commission seeks to identify the main trends influencing education bearing in mind economic growth and the aim of sustainable development; the transition front individual membership of a society to democratic participation; the relationship between the grass-roots community and world society.

The second part of the report lays emphasis on the imperative of quality in education and the concurrent need to satisfy the immense demand for education throughout the world. Resting on four main pillars - learning to know, learning to do, learning to be, and learning to live together - the learning process should be designed so as to enable every individual to develop by making the very most of his or her abilities. The concept of education can then be enlarged in time and in the social space to embrace that of learning throughout life.

Broadening the spectrum of educational opportunity, involving new actors in the educational process and creating closer links between the different types of education are prerequisites for success. We need to avoid a widening of the gap between a privileged minority of those who generally benefit from progress and substantial proportion of humankind left to suffer its drawbacks.

A questionnaire was sent to all the National Commission of UNESCO to invite submissions in the form of existing documentation or fresh material: the response was very positive, and the replies were studied carefully. Non-governmental organizations were similarly consulted and in some cases invited to participate in meetings.

In the third part of its report the Commission draws conclusions for educational processes from both the overall analysis and the central theme of learning throughout life, which is the key for equality of opportunity. The first teachers of a child, normally, are its parents; throughout youth and adulthood, learning takes place in a variety of forms: at school, in community life, the family, leisure pursuits, associations and civic life. This increasingly complex reality must be taken into account by all the actors in society in building on the four pillars of the learnings process. There is, needless to say, growing influence of information technologies that must be considered.

But it is within the education system - defined on traditional lines - that the central message is forged concerning the type of citizens a society wishes to educate, and that the continuity and progress of knowledge should be ensured. And, by extension, it is teachers who play the crucial, central role in maintaining the vigour of the system

***

Marshalling the components of the education process is not easy. It is difficult to define strategies, and still more difficult to implement them with all concerned. But it is precisely the responsibility of public policy, of government, to propose the direction to be followed, and to enlist the greatest possible number of actors in order to succeed in a strategy that masters change, both deliberate and inevitable.

***

Broadening the spectrum of educational opportunity, involving new actors in the educational process and creating closer links between the different types of education are prerequisites for success. We need to avoid a widening of the gap between a privileged minority of those who generally benefit from progress and a substantial proportion of humankind left to suffer its drawbacks.

The view taken in the Commission's report, which is not so much a review as the starting-point of a forward-looking debate, is one of committed optimism, and of voluntarism. It assumes that a certain number of human values- the dignity and responsibility of the individual, the free chosen participation of individuals in communities, equality of opportunity, the search for a common good—are universal, that they can be shared and applied collectively, and that education can play its part in this great enterprise.

By Way Of Conclusion

Considering the many challenges that the future holds in store, education appears to be an indispensable tool in humankind's attempt to attain the ideals of peace, freedom and social justice. As it concludes its work, the Commission states its belief that education plays a fundamental role in personal and social development. The Commission does not see education as a miracle cure or as the magic key to a world in which all ideals will be attained. In its view, education is nevertheless one of the principal means available to foster a deeper and more harmonious form of human development and thereby reduce poverty, exclusion, ignorance, oppression and war.

At a time when educational policies are being sharply criticized or pushed down on the list of economic and financial priorities the Commission wishes to share this conviction with the widest possible audience, through its analyses, discussions and recommendations. Our century has been noted as much for sound and fury as for economic and social progress—progress that in any case has not been equally shared. The dawn of a new century brings a prospect of anguish struggling with hope. It is essential in this context that all people with a sense of responsibility turn their attention to both the aims and the means of education. It is the view of the Commission that, while education is an ongoing process of improving one's knowledge and know-how, it is also—and perhaps primarily—the best means of bringing about personal development and building relationships among individuals, groups and nations.

This view was explicitly adopted by the members of the Commission when they accepted their mandate. They wished moreover, through their reflection to demonstrate the pivotal role of UNESCO. This role stems directly from the ideas on which UNESCO was founded, the hope for a world that is a better place to live in—where people will have learned to respect the rights of women and men, to show mutual understanding, and to use advances in knowledge to poster human development rather than to create further distinctions between people.

Our Commission had the doubtless impossible task of overcoming the obstacles presented by the extraordinary diversity of situations in the world and trying to arrive at analyses and conclusions that are generally valid and acceptable to everyone.

Nevertheless, the Commission did its best to project its thinking on to a future dominated by globalization, to ask the right questions and to lay down some broad guidelines that can be applied both within national contexts and on a global scale.

Looking Ahead

Some remarkable scientific discoveries and breakthrough have been made during the last twenty-five years. Many countries have ceased to be underdeveloped and are emerging; standards of living have continued to rise, albeit at paces that differ considerably from country to country. Despite this, the prevailing mood of disenchantment forms a sharp contrast with the hopes born in the years just after the Second World War.

The truth is that 'economic growth regardless' can no longer be viewed as the ideal way of reconciling material progress with equity, respect for the human condition and respect for the natural asset that we have a duty to hand on in good condition to future generations. Have we understood all the implications of this...?

One can, then, speak of disillusionment with economic and social progress. This is evident in rising unemployment and in the exclusion of growing numbers of people in the affluent countries. It is underscored by the continuing inequalities in development throughout the world[1]. While humankind is increasingly aware of the threats facing its natural environment, the resources needed to put matters right have not yet been allocated, despite a series of international meetings, such as the Rio Conference, and despite the serious warnings of natural disasters of or major industrial accidents. The truth is that 'economic growth regardless' can no longer be viewed as the ideal way of reconciling material progress with equity, respect for the human condition and respect for the natural assets that we have a duty to hand on in good condition to future generations.

Have we understood all the implications of this, both as regards the ends and means of sustainable development and for new forms of international co-operation? Certainly not! This will constitute one of the major intellectual and political challenges of the next century.

That being said, developing countries cannot disregard the classic forces driving growth, in particular participation in the domains of science and technology, with all this implies in terms of cultural adaptation and modernization of attitudes.

Those who felt that the end of Cold War held out the prospects of a better and more peaceful world have another reason for disenchantment and disillusionment. It is simply not an adequate consolation or excuse to repeat that history is tragic. That is something everyone knows or should know. Although the death toll in the last World War was fifty million, we must also remember that since 1945 some twenty million people have died in around 150 wars, started either before

1. *According to UNCTAD studies average income in the least-developed countries (560 million inhabitants) is falling. The estimated figure is $300 a year per inhabitant as against $906 for developing countries and $21,598 for the industrialized countries.*

or since the fall of the Berlin Wall. Are these new risks or old risks? That hardly matters. Tensions smoulder and then flare up between national and ethnic groups, or as a result of a build-up of social and economic injustices.

> *Tensions smoulder and their flare up between national and ethnic groups, or as a result of a build-up of social and economic injustices. Against a background of growing interdependence among peoples and the globalization of problems, decision-makers have a duty to assess these risks and take action to diminish them.*

Against a background of growing interdependence among peoples and the globalization of problems, decision-makers have a duty to assess these risks and take action to diminish them.

But how can we learn to live together in the global village if we cannot manage to live together in the communities to which we naturally belong—the nation, the region, the city, the village, the neighborhood? Do we want to make a contribution to public life and can we do so? That question is central to democracy. But we should not forget that the will to contribute must come from each person's sense of responsibility. Although democracy has won new territory in lands formerly in the grip of totalitarianism and despotic rule, it is showing signs of languishing in countries which have had democratic institutions for many decades. It is as if there is a constant need for new beginnings and as if everything has to be renewed or reinvented.

How could these major challenges not be a concern in educational policy making? How could the Commission fail to highlight the ways in which educational policies can help to create a better world, by contributing to sustainable human development, mutual, understanding among people and a renewal of practical democracy?

Overcoming the Tensions

To this end, we have to confront, and thus be better

able to overcome, the main tensions that although they are not new, will be central to they problems of the twenty-first century.

There is the tension between the global and the local; people need to become world citizens, without losing their roots while continuing to play an active part in the life of their national and their local community. Another tension exists between the universal and the individual: culture is steadily being globalized, but as yet only partially. We cannot ignore the promises of globalization nor its risks, including the tendency to forget the unique character of each human being. Yet, we are summoned to chose our future and achieve our full potential within the carefully tended wealth of our traditions and our own cultures which, unless we are careful, can be endangered by contemporary developments.

The tension between tradition and modernity is part of the same problem: how is it possible to adapt without turning one's back on the past, how can one acquire independence in complementarity with the free development of others and how can one master scientific progress? It is in this spirit that the challenge of the new information technologies must be met.

We cannot ignore the promises of globalization nor its risks, including the tendency to forget the unique character of each human being. Yet, we are summoned to choose our future and achieve our full potential within the carefully tended wealth of our traditions and our own cultures which, unless we are careful, can be endangered by contemporary developments.

Long-term and sort-term considerations have always been in conflict. Today, however, this tension is sustained by the prevalence of the ephemeral and the instantaneous in a world where an over-abundance of information and fleeting emotion continually keeps the spotlight on immediate problems Public opinion cries out for quick answers and ready solutions, whereas often what is called for is a patient, concerted, negotiated reform strategy. This is precisely the case where education policies are concerned.

A further source of tension exists between, on the one hand, the need for competition, and on the other the concern for equality of opportunity. This is a perennial issue, which has been facing both economic and social policy-makers since the beginning of the century. Although it has sometimes been resolved, enduring answers have never been found. Today, the Commission ventures to claim that the pressures of competitiveness have driven many authorities to lose sight of their mission, which is to give each human being the means to take full advantage of every opportunity. This has led us, within the terms of reference of the report, to rethink and update the concept of life long education so as to reconcile three forces: competition, which provides incentives; co-operation which gives strength; and solidarity which unites.

Lastly, there is the age-old tension between the spiritual and the material. Although not always overtly felt or expressed, there is thirst for ideals and values which we shall term 'moral ideals and values' to avoid offending anyone. Education has the noble task of stimulating in everyone, in accordance with their traditions and convictions, and with full regard for pluralism, an elevation of thought and mind reaching out to the universal and a measure of self-transcendence. The survival of humanity - and the Commission does not say this lightly - hinges on this.

Designing and Building our Common Future

Our contemporaries feel torn between a globalization whose manifestations they can see and sometimes have to bear, their search for roots, reference points and a sense of belonging.

It is through education that we can comprehend the painful birth of a world society. Thus education will play a central role in both personal and community development. Its mission is to enable each of us, without exception, to develop all our talents and creative potential, including the responsibility for our own lives and achievement of our goals.

This aim is more important than all other educational aims. Although it will take a long period of hard work to achieve, it will be an essential contribution to the search for a more just world, a better world to live in. The Commission wishes to stress this point, at a time when serious doubts are being expressed about the opportunities opened up by education.

Many other problems clearly have to be solved, and we shall come back to them. But, this report has been prepared at a moment when, faced with so many misfortunes caused by war, crime and underdevelopment, humankind is apparently hesitating between continuing headlong the same path or resignation. Let us offer people another way.

This way leads to a renewed emphasis on the moral and cultural dimensions of education. It means enabling each person to grasp the individuality of other people and to understand the chaotic move of the world towards a certain unity. But it begins with self-understanding through an inner voyage, whose milestones are knowledge, meditation and the spirit of self-criticism.

> *This report has been prepared at a moment when, faced with so many misfortunes caused by war, crime and underdevelopment, humankind is apparently hesitating between continuing headlong along the same path or resignation. Let us offer people another way. This way leads to a renewed emphasis on the moral and cultural dimensions of education.*

This message should guide educational thinking, in conjunction with the establishment of wider and more far-reaching forms of international co-operation which will be discussed in the final part of these conclusions.

Things fall into place in such a perspective, whether we are considering the requirements of science and technology, knowledge of self and of the environment, or the development of skills enabling each person to function effectively in a family, as a citizen or as a productive member of society.

The Commission in no way undervalues the central role of intellectual endeavour and innovation, at a moment when the endogenous processes that make it possible to accumulate knowledge, to incorporate new discoveries and to apply them in different areas of human activity, from those related to health and the environment to the production of goods and services, are effecting a transition to a knowledge-driven society. It is also aware of the limits, and even the failures, of attempts to transfer technologies to the most impoverished countries, precisely because of the endogenous nature of the accumulation and application of knowledge. It is for this reason, among others, that it is important to become familiar at an early age with science and the uses of science and with the difficult task of controlling progress in such a way that human identity and integrity are fully respected. Here, too, the ethical issues must not be overlooked.

The Commission is also aware of the contribution that education must make to economic and social development. The education system is all too often blamed for unemployment. This observation is only partly true; above all it should not obscure the other political, economic and social prerequisites for achieving full employment or enabling the economies of underdeveloped countries to take off. As for education, the Commission believes that valid responses to the problems of mismatch between supply and demahd on the labour market can come from a more flexible system that allows greater curricular diversity and builds bridges between different types of education; or offers sandwich course or job release schemes. Such flexibility would also help to reduced school failure and the tremendous wastage of human potential resulting from it.

> *The Commission is also aware of contribution that education must make to economic and social development. The education system is all too often blamed for unemployment. This observation is only partly true; above all it should not obscure the other political, economic and social prerequisites for achieving full employment or enabling the economies of underdeveloped countries to take off*

Improvements, however, desirable and feasible, do not obviate the need for intellectual innovation and the implementation of a model of sustainable development based on the specific needs of each country. Given the present and foreseeable advance in science and technology and the growing importance of knowledge and other intangible inputs in the production of goods and services, we need to rethink the place of work and its changing status in tomorrow's society. To create tomorrow's society, imagination will have to keep ahead of technological breakthroughs in order to avoid further increases in unemployment and social exclusion or inequalities in development.

For all these reasons, it seems to us that the concept of an education pursued throughout life, with all its advantages in terms of flexibility, diversity and availability to persons at different times and in different places, should command wide support. There is a need to rethink and broaden the notion of lifelong education. More than adapting to changes in work, education throughout life should also constitute a continuous forging of one's own personality—one's knowledge and aptitudes, but also the critical faculty and the ability to act. It should enable people to develop awareness of themselves and their environment and encourage full participation in work and society.

In this context, the Commission discussed the need to advance towards 'a learning society'. The truth is that every aspect of life, at both the individual and social level, offers opportunities for both learning and doing. One could be tempted to focus too much on the general availability of such learning opportunities, stressing the educational potential of the modern media, the world of work or cultural and leisure pursuits, even to the extent of forgetting a number of fundamental truths. Although people need to use all opportunities for learning and self-improvement, they will not be able to make good use of all these potential resources unless they have received a sound basic education. School should impart both the desire for and pleasure in learning, the ability to learn how to learn, and intellectual curiosity. One might even imagine a society in which each individual would be in turn both teacher and learner.

The basis for a learning society is formal education system, where each individual is introduced to the many different forms of knowledge. There is no substitute for the teacher - pupil relationship, which is underpinned by authority and developed through dialogue. This has been argued time and time again by the great classical thinkers who have studied the question of education. It is the responsibility of the teacher to impart to the pupil the knowledge that humankind has acquired about itself and about nature, and the essence of human creativity and inventiveness.

Although people need to use all opportunities for learning and self-improvement, they will not be able to make good use of all these potential resources unless they have received a sound basic education. School should impart both the desire for and pleasure in, learning, the ability to learn how to learn, and intellectual curiosity. One might even imagine a society in which each individual would be in turn both teacher and learner.

Learning Throughout Life: The Heartbeat of Society

The concept of learning throughout life is one of the keys to the twenty-first century. It goes beyond the traditional distinction between initial schooling and continuing education. It meets the challenges posed by a rapidly changing world. This is not a new insight, since previous reports on education have emphasized the need for people to return to education in order to deal with new situations that occur in their personal and working lives. The need, though, is still felt and is even becoming stronger. The only way of satisfying it is for each individual to learn how to learn. But there is a further requirement: the far-reaching changes in the traditional patterns of human existence require of us a better understanding of other people and the world at large. These is a need for mutual understanding, peaceful interchange and, indeed, harmony —the very things that are most lacking in our world today.

This position leads the Commission to put greater emphasis on one of the four pillars that it has proposed and described as the foundations of education. This involves learning to live together, by developing an understanding of others and their history, traditions and spirituality. It would provide a basis for the creation of a new spirit which, guided by recognition of our growing interdependence and a common analysis of the risks and challenges of the future, would induce people to implement common projects or to manage the inevitable conflicts in an intelligent and peaceful way. Utopia, one might argue; yet is a necessary Utopia, indeed a vital one if we are to escape from a dangerous cycle sustained by cynicism and complacency.

Yes, the Commission has a vision of the kind of education that will breed this new spirit. But it has not disregarded the three other pillars of education which provide, as it were, the bases for learning to live together.

The first of these is **learning to know**. Bearing in mind the rapid changes brought about by scientific progress and the new forms of economic and social activity, the emphasis has to be on combining a sufficiently broad general education with the possibility of in-depth work on a selected number of subjects. Such a general education is basically the passport to learning throughout life, in so far as it should teach people to enjoy learning and also lay the foundations that will enable them to carry on learning throughout their lives.

> *Bearing in mind the rapid changes brought about by scientific progress and the new forms of economic and social activity, the emphasis has to be on combining a sufficiently broad general education with the possibility in-depth work on a selected number of subjects. Such a general education is basically the passport to learning throughout life...*

Learning to do is another pillar. In addition to learning to practise a profession or trade, people need to develop the ability to face a variety of situations, often unforeseeable, and to work in teams a feature of educational methods that does not at present receive enough attention. In many cases, such competence and skill are more readily acquired if pupils and students have the opportunity to develop their abilities by becoming involved in work experience schemes or social work while they are still in education. Therefore, increased importance should be attached to all schemes in which education alternates with work.

Last, but far from least, is the fourth pillar, **learning to be**. This was the theme of the Edgar Faure report published under the auspices of UNESCO in 1972. Its recommendations are still extremely relevant, for in the twenty-first century, everyone will need to exercise greater independence and judgement combined with stronger sense of personal responsibility for the attainment of common goals. Our report stresses a further imperative: none of the talents which are hidden like buried treasure in every person must be left untapped. These are, to name but a few; memory, reasoning power, imagination, physical ability, aesthetic sense, the aptitude to communicate with each others, and the natural charisma of the group leader. They lead to the obligation to better understand one's own personality.

None of the talents which are hidden like buried treasure in every person must be left untapped. These are, to name but a few: memory, reasoning power, imagination, physical ability, aesthetic sense, the aptitude to communicate with each others, and the natural charisma of the group leader. They lead to the obligation to better understand one's own personality.

The Commission has alluded to another Utopian idea: a learning society founded on the acquisition, the renewal and the use of knowledge. These are three aspects that ought to be emphasized in the educational process. Now, when the development of the 'information society' is increasing opportunities for access to data and facts, education should enable everyone to gather information and to select, arrange, manage and use it.

Education should therefore constantly adapt to changes in society, but it must not fail to pass on the attainments, foundations and benefits of human experience, either.

Faced then with a growing demand for education in both quantity and quality, how can education policies achieve the twin aims of high educational standards and equity? These were the questions that the Commission addressed concerning courses of study, educational methods and content, and prerequisites for the effectiveness of education.

The Stages and Bridges of Learning : A Fresh Approach

By focussing on the concept of learning throughout life, the Commission did not intend to convey the idea that by a qualitative leap one could avoid reflecting on the different levels of education. One the contrary, it intended, on the one hand, to reassert some principles advanced by UNESCO, such as the vital need for basic education. On the other, it wished to urge a review of the role of secondary education, and to examine issues emerging from changes in higher education, particularly the development of mass higher education.

Quite simply, learning throughout life permits a re-ordering of the sequences and itineraries of education, easier passage from one stage to another and recognition of the value of each. Thus can be avoided the invidious dilemma of deciding between selective education, which increases the number of educational failures and the risks of exclusion, and comprehensive education, which can inhibit talent.

Quite simply, learning throughout life permits reordering of the sequences and itineraries of education, easier passage from one stage to another and recognition of the value of each. Thus can be avoided the invidious dilemma of deciding between selective education, which increases the number of educational failures and the risks of exclusion, and comprehensive education, which can inhibit talent.

This focus in no way reduces the significance of the excellent definition of basic leaning needs produced in 1990 at the Jomtien Conference on Education for All.

'These needs comprise both essential learning tools (such as literacy, oral expression, numeracy and problem solving) and the basic learning content (such as knowledge, skills, values and attitudes) required by human beings to be able to survive, to develop their full capacities to live and work in dignity, to participate fully in development, to improve the quality of their lives, to make informed decisions, and to continue learning.'

This is certainly an impressive catalogue. We should conclude, though, that it leads to a proliferation of courses. The teacher-pupil relationship, the learning available in children's local community, and an effective use of modern communications media (where they exist) can in concert make a contribution to the personal and intellectual development of each pupil. The 'three Rs'-reading, writing and arithmetic-get their full due. The combination of conventional teaching and out-of-school approaches should enable children to experience the three dimensions of education - the moral and cultural, the scientific and technological, and the economic and social.

Education is also a social experience through which children learn about themselves, develop interpersonal skills and acquire basic knowledge and skills. This experience should begin in early childhood, in different forms depending on the situation, but always involving families and local communities.

Two observations, which the Commission sees as important, should be added at this stage.

Basic education should be provided worldwide for 900 million illiterate adults, 130 million children not enrolled in school, and more than 100 million children who drop out prematurely. This vast undertaking is a priority for technical assistance and partnership carried out through international co-operation.

Basic education is of course an issue in all countries, including the industrialized ones. It should be designed to stimulate a love of learning and knowledge and thus the desire and opportunities for education later in life.

We must also consider one of the major problem areas in any reform: the policies aimed at the period of adolescence and youth between primary education and work or higher education. **Secondary schools** are, as it were, neglected in educational thinking. They are the target of considerable criticism, and they provoke a considerable amount of frustration.

Among the sources of frustration is a demand for expansion and diversification of secondary education, leading to rapid growth in enrolments and overcrowded curricula. There emerge well-known problems associated with mass education, which largely underdeveloped countries cannot easily solve at either the financial or the organizational level. Furthermore, there is the discouraging problem of school levers who face a shortage of opportunities, their distress increased by a widespread all-or-nothing obsession with access to higher education. Mass unemployment in many countries can only add to the malaise. The Commission stresses its alarm at a trend that is leading, in both rural and urban areas, in both developing and industrialized countries, not only to unemployment but also to the under-utilization of human resources.

> *Basic education should be provided worldwide for 900 million illiterate adults 130 million children not enrolled in school, and more than 100 million children who drop out prematurely. This vast undertaking is a priority for technical assistance and partnership carried out through international co-operation. Basic education of course an issue in all countries, including the industrialized ones....*

The Commission is convinced that the only way out of this difficult situation is a very broad diversification of types of study available. This reflects one of the Commission's major concerns, which is showing the value of all forms of talent so as to reduce school failure and prevent the far-too-widespread feeling among young people that they are excluded, with no future in store.

Types of secondary education should include both conventional education which focuses more on abstraction and conceptualization- and approaches that combine school and job experience in a way that brings out additional abilities and inclinations. In any event, there should be bridges between these approaches so that errors in choice of direction - all too frequent- can be corrected.

Furthermore, the prospect of being able to go back to education or training would, in the view of the Commission, alter the general climate by assuring each young person that his or her fate is not sealed between the age of 14 and 20.

Higher education should be seen from this same angle.

Let us remember that side by with universities, there are other types of higher education institutions in many countries. Some are highly selective, while others were set up to provide specifically targeted, quality professional and vocational training, lasting between two and four years. Such diversification obviously meets the needs of society and the economy, both at the national and regional levels.

Increasingly stringent selection in order to ease the pressures brought about by mass higher education, in the wealthiest countries is neither politically nor socially acceptable. Adopting such an approach creates a new problem: many young people are expelled from the educational process before they have been able to obtain a recognized diploma; they are therefore in the desperate predicament of having neither a degree nor training appropriate for the job market.

There is a need to manage increasing enrolment, but increases can be limited as a result of secondary education reform, along the broad lines proposed by the Commission.

Universities would contribute to this process by diversifying what they offer:

- as scientific establishments and centres of learning, leading to theoretical or applied research or teaching;
- as establishments offering professional qualification, combining high level academic knowledge and skill development, with course and content continually tailored to the need of the economy;
- as one of the main crossroads for learning throughout life, opening the way to adults who wish to return to

education either to adapt and develop their knowledge or to satisfy their taste for learning in all areas of cultural life;

- as leading partners in international co-operation, favouring exchanges of teachers and students, and promoting dissemination of first-class teaching through international professorships.

Increasingly stringent selection in order to ease the pressures brought about by mass higher education, in the wealthiest countries, is neither politically nor socially acceptable. Adopting such an approach creates a new problem: many young people are expelled from the educational process before they have been able to obtain a recognized diploma; they are therefore in the desperate predicament of having neither a degree nor training appropriate for the job market.

In this way, universities would transcend the needless opposition between public service and the rest of the job market. They would also reclaim their intellectual and social vocation as, in a sense, one of the guarantors of universal values and cultural heritage. The Commission sees this as a cogent reason for greater university autonomy.

Having formulated these proposals, the Commission emphasizes that these countries, universities must learn from their own pasts, and analyze the difficulties around them, engaging in research aimed at finding solutions to the most acute among them. It is also incumbent on them to propose a renewed vision of development that will enable their countries to build a genuinely better future. They must aim to provide the vocational and technological training of the future leaders, and the graduate and post-graduate education required if their countries are to escape from their present treadmills of poverty and underdevelopment. It is particularly necessary to devise new development models for regions such as sub-Saharan Africa, as has already been done on an individual basis by the Eastern Asian countries.

Getting the Reform Strategies Right

One should not underestimate the obligation to manage short-term constraints or disregard the need to adapt existing systems. The Commission wishes, though, to emphasize the need for a more longterm approach if the reforms required are to succeed. By the same token, it stresses the fact that reforms one after another cancel out each other, since they do not allow the system the time needed either to absorb change or to get all actors involved in the process. Furthermore, past failures show that many reformers adopt an approach that is either too radical or too theoretical, ignoring what can be usefully learned from experience, and rejecting past achievements. As a result, teachers, parents and pupils are disoriented and less than willing to accept and implement reform.

Three main actors contribute to the success of educational reforms: first of all, the local community, including parents, school heads and teachers; but also the public authorities; and the international community. Much past failure has been due to insufficient involvement of one or more of these partners. Attempts to impose educational reforms from the top down, or from outside, have obviously failed. Countries where the process has been relatively successful are those that obtained a determined commitment from local communities, parents and teachers, backed up by continuing dialogue and various forms of financial, technical and/or vocational assistance. It is obvious that the local community plays a paramount role in any successful reform strategy.

Local community participation in assessing needs by means of a dialogue with the public authorities and groups concerned in society is a first, essential stage in broadening access to education and improving its quality. Continuing the dialogue by way of the media, community discussions, parent education and training, and on-the-job teacher training, usually arouses greater awareness, develops judgement and helps build local capacities. When communities assume greater responsibility for their own development, they learn to appreciate the role of education both in achieving societal objectives and in improving the quality of life.

Here the commission stresses the great advantages of prudent decentralization in helping to increase responsibility and the ability to innovate at the school level.

In any event, no reform can succeed without the cooperative and active participation of the teachers. For the Commission, this is one way of recommending that the social, cultural and material status of educators should be considered as a matter of priority.

> *In any event, no reform can succeed without the cooperative and active participation of the teachers. For the Commission, this is one way of the recommending that the social, cultural and material status of educators should be considered as a matter of priority. We are asking a great deal, too much even, of teachers, when we expect them to make good the failings of other institutions which also have a responsibility for the education and training of young people.*

We are asking a great deal, too much even of teachers, when we expect them to make good the failings of other institutions which also have a responsibility for the education and training of young people. The demands made on teachers are considerable, at the very time when the outside world is reaching increasingly into the school, particularly through the new communication and information media. The young people with whom the teacher has to deal are under less supervision than in the past by their families or religious movements, but they are also better informed. Teachers have to take this new situation into account if they are to be heard and understood by young people. They must impart to them an inclination for learning, and show them that information and knowledge are two different things, and that knowledge requires effort, concentration, discipline and determination.

Rightly or wrongly, teachers feel isolated, not just because teaching is an individual act, but also because of the expectations aroused by education and the criticisms which are often unjustly directed at them. Above all teachers want to see their dignity respected. Most teachers are members of unions—in some cases, powerful unions—which are undeniably committed to the protection of their corporate interests. Even so, there is a need for the dialogue between society and teachers and between the public authorities and teachers unions to be both strengthened and seen in new light.

Let us recognize that the renewal of this kind of dialogue is no easy task. Renewal is essential, however, in order to put an end to the teachers' feelings of isolation and frustration, and to make change acceptable and ensure that everyone contributes to the success of the necessary reforms.

Fully aware of classroom practicalities today, the Commission lays great emphasis on the quantity and quality of traditional teaching materials, in particular books, and on new media, such as information technologies, which should be used with discernment and with active pupil participation. For their part, teachers should work in teams, particularly in secondary schools, thereby helping to achieve the necessary flexibility.

In this context, it is appropriate to add some recommendations concerning the content of teacher training, the access of all teachers to continuing education, and greater involvement of teachers in disadvantaged and marginalized groups, where they can help to improve the integration of children and adolescents in society.

This is also a plea for providing the education system not only with well-trained teachers but also with the tools required to deliver education of a high standard. These tools should include books, modern communication media, and suitable cultural and economic support for the school.

Fully aware of classroom practicalities today, the Commission lays great emphasis on the quantity and quality of traditional teaching materials, in particular books, and on new media, such as information technologies, which should be used with discernment and with active pupil participation. For their part, teachers should work in teams, particularly in secondary schools, thereby helping to achieve the necessary flexibility. This can avoid failures, bringing out some of the pupils' natural talents and providing better study and career guidance with a view to learning continued throughout life.

Given the above, improving education systems requires responsible public policy. Policy-makers cannot assume that the market can compensate for the failures in the system or that laisserfaire is sufficient.

It is on the strength of its belief in the importance of public policy that the Commission has stressed the permanence of values, the challenges of future demands, preparing the future, and review of the duties of teachers and society. It is through policy formulation that vital public discussions can be generated and all issues considered. Education is everyone's business: our future is at stake, and it is through education that one can seek to improve the lives of all people.

The Commission noted the growing need, in the political and economic spheres, to resort to international action as a way of finding satisfactory solutions to problems that have a global dimension, if for no other reason than the growing interdependence so often emphasized. It also regretted the inadequacy of results and stressed the need for reform of international institutions to make their action more effective.

This naturally leads us to focus on the role of the public authorities. They must propose clear options and, after broad consultation with all those involved, choose polices that, regardless of whether the education system is State, private or mixed, give the direction, prepare the system's foundation and main features and regulate the system through the necessary adjustments.

Naturally, all public policy decisions have financial repercussions. The Commission does not underestimate this difficulty. Without entering into the complexities of various systems, it holds the view that education is a public good and should be available to all people. Once this principle is accepted, public and private funding may be combined, according to different formulae that take into account each country's traditions, stage of development, ways of life and forms of income distribution. But whatever the case may be, all the choices to be made should be predicated upon the fundamental principle of equal opportunity.

During the discussions, the Chairman of the Commission put forward a more radical proposal. As education throughout life gradually becomes reality, all young persons could be allocated an education voucher at the start of their education. This would entitle them to a certain number of years of education. This entitlement would be credited to an account at a bank which would manage a capital of time available for each individual, together with the appropriate funds. Everyone could use their capital for schooling, on the basis of their own choices. Some of the capital could be set aside to enable people to receive continuing education during their adult lives. Each person could increase his or her capital through deposits at the bank under a king of educational savings scheme. After thorough discussion, the Commission supported this idea, though it was aware of potential deviations, to the detriment even of equality of opportunity. Thus, given present-day realities, the education voucher might be allocated at the end of compulsory schooling so as to enable adolescents to choose a path without jeopardizing future choices.

Broadening International Co-operation in the Global Village

The Commission noted the growing need, in the

political and economic spheres, to resort to international action as a way of finding satisfactory solutions to problems that have a global dimension, if for no other reason than the growing interdependence so often emphasized. It also regretted the inadequacy of results and stressed the need for reform of international institutions to make their action more effective. There is need for effective action in both the social and the educational fields. The importance of the world Summit on Social Development, held in Copenhagen in March 1995, has been deliberately stressed. Education occupies a prominent place in the guidelines adopted.

The Commission framed a number of recommendations concerning:

- a Policy of strong encouragement for the education of girls and women, following on the recommendations of the Beijing Conference held in September 1995;
- the allocation of a minimum percentage of development aid (a quarter of the total) to fund education: this adjustment in favour of education should also apply to international funding institutions, first and foremost the World Bank, which already has an important role;
- the further development of debt-for-education swaps to offset the adverse effects on State education expenditure of adjustment policies and policies for reducing internal and external deficits;
- the widespread introduction of the new technologies of the 'information society' in all countries, to prevent the growth of yet another gap between rich countries and poor countries;
- enlisting the outstanding potential of non-governmental organization, naturally including grass-roots initiatives, which can provide valuable support to international co-operation in education.

These few suggestions should be seen in the context

of partnership rather than aid. After so many failures and so much waste, experience militates in favour of partnership. Globalization makes it inescapable. There are some encouraging examples such as the successful co-operation and exchanges within regional groupings, the European Union being a case in point.

> *After so many failures and so much waste, experience militates in favour of partnership. Globalization makes it inescapable. There are some encouraging examples such as the successful co-operation and exchanges within regional groupings, the European Union being a case in point.*

Another justification for the partnership approach is that it can lead to a 'win-win situation'. Whist industrialized countries can assist developing countries by contributing their successful experiences, their technologies and financial and material resources, developing countries can teach the industrialized countries ways of passing on their cultural heritage, approaches to the socialization of children and, more fundamentally, different cultures and ways of life.

The Commission expresses the hope that the Member States will give UNESCO the necessary resources to enable it to foster partnership, both in spirit and in reality, along the lines suggested by the Commission to the General Conference.

UNESCO can do this by making known successful innovations and helping to establish networks on the basis of grass-roots initiatives by NGOs, designed both to develop education of a high standard (UNESCO Chairs) and to stimulate research partnerships.

More fundamentally, however, UNESCO will serve peace and mutual understanding among people by continuing to stress the value of education as a means of reconciliation and a way to develop the will to live together, as active members of our global village, thinking and organizing for the good of future generations. It is in this way that UNESCO will contribute to a culture of peace.

> *Another justification for the partnership approach is that it can lead to a 'win-win situation'. Whist industrialized countries can assist developing countries by contributing their successful experiences, their technologies and financial and material resources, developing countries can teach the industrialized countries ways of passing on their cultural heritage, approaches to the socialization of children and, more fundamentally, different cultures and ways of life.*

(Source: DPEP Calling, January 1996.)

4

Learning : The Treasure Within

—Report to UNESCO of the International Commission on Education for the Twenty-first Century

Learning : The Treasure Within, *the report to UNESCO of the International Commission on Education for the Twenty-first Century, is the result of a three year worldwide process of consultation and analysis carried out by a distinguished panel of specialists under the chairmanship of Mr. Jacques Delors, former President of the European Commission. It is a thought provoking one that proposes ideas that go far beyond mere educational reform: it examines the place and functions of education in relation to individual achievement and social development in a changing world.*

Education is one of the principal means available to foster a deeper and more harmonious form of human development and thereby to reduce poverty, exclusion, ignorance, oppression and war. The coming century, dominated by globalization, also means that education will have to adapt itself to considerable economic, social and cultural changes resulting in inevitable tensions between tradition and modernity, competition and equality of opportunity, spiritual aspirations and material reality, local interests and global considerations, the unlimited expansion of knowledge and the limited capacity of human beings to assimilate it. In this context, learning throughout life will play a key role in meeting the challenges of the next century.

Building on the four pillars that constitute the foundations of education — *learning to be, learning to know, learning to do and learning to live together* - all societies should move towards a necessary Utopia in which none of the talents hidden like buried treasure in every person are left untapped. Based on a new outlook on education and a fresh approach to the learning process, the report proposes more flexible education systems, where the value of each individual is enhanced. As such, while universal basic education is an absolute priority, secondary education has a pivotal role in the learning process of young people and social development. Higher education institutions should become not only centres of knowledge and places for professional training, but also the crossroads for learning throughout life and the privileged arena for international co-operation.

The central role of teachers and the need to improve their training, status and conditions of work is particularly stressed. In a world increasingly dominated by technology, emphasis is placed on the use of technology in the service of education and adequate training for later use at work and in daily life. Innovative guidelines are set out for educational renewal, based on strategies of education reforms which take into account a broad-based dialogue, and by increasing responsibility and involvement of stakeholders at every level. The report closes with a strong plea for more resources to be devoted to education, both nationally and internationally, and for strengthening international co-operation in education, with UNESCO as a key player.

The *pointers* identified and *recommendations* made in the "Learning: The Treasure Within" by the International Commission on Education for the Twenty-first century are explained here under :

1. From the Local Community to a World Society

Worldwide interdependence and globalization are major forces in contemporary life. They are already at work and will leave a deep imprint on the twenty-first century. They require that overall consideration, extending well beyond the fields of education and culture, be given, as of now, to the roles and structures of international organizations.

The major danger is that of a gulf opening up between a minority of people who are capable of finding their way successfully about this new world that is coming into being and the majority who feel that they are at the mercy of events and have no say in the future of society, with the dangers that entails of a setback to democracy and widespread revolt

We must be guided by the Utopian aim of steering the world towards greater mutual understanding, a greater sense of responsibility and greater solidarity, through acceptance of our spiritual and cultural differences. Education, by providing access to knowledge for all, has precisely this universal task of helping people to understand the world and to understand others.

2. From Social Cohesion to Democratic Participation

Education policy must be sufficiently diversified and must be so designed as not to become another contributory cause of social exclusion.

The socialization of individuals must not conflict with personal development. It is therefore necessary to work towards a system that strives to combine the virtues of integration with respect for individual rights.

Education cannot, on its own, solve the problems raised by the severance (when this happens) of social ties. It can, however, be expected to help to foster the desire to live together, which is a basic component of social cohesion and national identity.

Schools cannot succeed in this task unless they make their own contribution to the advancement and integration of minority groups by mobilizing those concerned while showing due regard for their personality.

Democracy appears to be progressing, taking forms and passing through stages that fit the situation in each country. Its vitality is nevertheless constantly threatened. Education for conscious and active citizenship must begin at school.

Democratic participation is, so to say, a matter of good citizenship, but it can be encouraged or stimulated by instruction and practices adapted to a media and information society. What is needed is to provide reference points an aids to interpretation, so as to strengthen the faculties of understanding and judgement.

It is the role of education to provide children and adults with the cultural background that will enable them, as far as possible, to make sense of the changes taking place. This presupposes that they are capable of sorting the mass of information so as to interpret it more effectively and place events in a historical perspective.

3. From Economic Growth to Human Development

Further reflection on the theme of a new model of development, showing more respect for nature and the structuring of people's time.

A future oriented study of the place of work in society, taking into account the effects of technical progress and change on both private and community life.

A fuller assessment of development, taking all its aspects into account, along the lines of the work done by UNDP.

The establishment of new links between educational policy and development policy, with a view to strengthening the bases of knowledge and skills in the countries concerned: encouragement of initiative, teamwork, realistic synergies taking local resources into account, self-employment and the spirit of enterprise.

The necessary improvement and general availability of basic education (importance of the Jomtien Declaration).

4. The Four Pillars of Education

Education throughout life is based on four pillars : learning to know, learning to do, learning to live together and learning to be.

Learning to Know, by combining a sufficiently broad general knowledge with the opportunity to work in depth on a small number of subjects. This also means learning to learn, so as to benefit from the opportunities education provides throughout life.

Learning to do, in order to acquire not only an occupational skill but also, more broadly, the competence to deal with many situations and work in teams. It also means learning to do in the context of young peoples' various social and work experiences which may be informal, as a result of the local or national context or formal, involving courses, alternating study and work.

Learning to live together, by developing an understanding of other people and an appreciation of interdependence—carrying out joint projects and learning to manage conflicts in a spirit of respect for the values of pluralism, mutual understanding and peace.

Learning to be, so as better to develop one's personality and be able to act with every greater autonomy, judgement and personal responsibility. In that connection, education must not disregard any aspect of a person's potential: memory, reasoning, aesthetic sense, physical capacities and communication skills.

Formal education systems tend to emphasize the acquisition of knowledge to the detriment of other types of learning: but it is vital now to conceive education in a more encompassing fashion. Such a vision should inform and guide future educational reforms and policy, in relation both to contents and to methods.

5. Learning Through Life

The concept of learning through life is the key that gives access to the twenty-first century. It goes beyond the traditional distinction between initial and continuing education. It links up with another concept often put forward, that of the learning society, in which everything affords an opportunity of learning and fulfilling one's potential.

In its new guise, continuing education is seen as going far beyond what is already practised, particularly in the developed countries, i.e. upgrading, with refresher training, retraining and conversion or promotion courses for adults. It should open up opportunities for learning for all, for many different purposes - offering them a second or third chance, satisfying their desire for knowledge and beauty or their desire to surpass themselves, or making it possible to broaden and deepen strictly vocational forms of training, including practical training.

In short, 'learning throughout life' must take advantage of all the opportunities offered by society.

6. From Basic Education to University

A requirement valid for all countries, albeit in various forms and with different types of content - the *strengthening of basic education* : hence the emphasis on *primary education* and its traditional basic programmes - reading, writing, arithmetic - but also on the ability to express oneself in a language that lends itself to dialogue and understanding.

The need, which will be still greater tomorrow, for receptivity to science and the world of science, which opens the door to the twenty-first century and its scientific and technological upheavals.

The adaptation of *basic education* to specific contexts, the most deprived countries as well as the most deprived section of the population, starting out with the facts of everyday life, which affords opportunities for understanding natural phenomena and for different forms of socialization.

The pressing needs of literacy work and basic education for adults are to be kept in mind.

In all cases, emphasis is to be placed on pupil-teacher relations, since the most advanced technologies can be no more than a back-up to the relationship (transmission, dialogue and confrontation) between teacher and pupil.

Secondary education must be rethought in this general context of learning throughout life. The key principle is to arrange for a variety of individual paths through schooling, without ever closing the door on the possibility of a subsequent return to the education system.

Debates on selection and guidance would be greatly clarified if this principle were fully applied. Everyone would then feel that whatever the choices made or the courses followed in adolescence, no doors would ever be closed in the future, including the doors of the school itself. Equality of opportunity would then mean what it says.

Universities should be central to the higher level of the system, even if, as is the case in many countries, there are other, non-university establishments of higher education.

Universities would have vested in them four key functions : 1. To prepare students for research and teaching. 2. To provide highly specialized training courses adapted to the needs of economic and social life. 3. To be open to all, so as to cater for the many aspects of lifelong education in the widest sense. 4. International co-operation.

The universities should also be able to speak out on ethical and social problems as entirely independent and fully responsible institutions exercising a kind of intellectual authority that society needs to help it to reflect, understand and act.

The diversity of secondary schooling and the possibilities afforded by universities should provide a valid answer to the challenges of mass education by dispelling the obsession with a one-and-only educational 'king's highway'. Combined with more widespread application of the practice of alternating periods of education with periods of work, these approaches can provide effective tools for fighting against school failure. The extension of learning throughout life will require consideration of new procedures for certification that take account of acquired competences.

7. Teachers in Search of New Perspectives

While the psychological and material situation of teachers differs greatly from country to country, an upgrading of their status is essential if 'learning throughout life' is to fulfil the central function assigned to it by the Commission in the advancement of our societies and the strengthening of mutual understanding among peoples. Their position as master or mistress in the classroom should be recognized by society and they should be given the necessary authority and suitable resources.

The concept of learning throughout life leads straight on to that of a learning society, a society that offers many and varied opportunities of learning, both at school and in economic, social and cultural life, whence the need for more collaboration and partnerships with families, industry and business, voluntary associations, people active in cultural life, etc.

Teachers are also concerned by the imperative requirement to update knowledge and skills. Their professional lives should be so arranged as to accommodate the opportunity, or even the obligation, for them to become more proficient in their art and to benefit from periods of experience in various spheres of economic, social and cultural life. Such possibilities are usually provided for in the many forms of study leave or sabbatical leave. Those formulae, suitably adapted, should be extended to all teachers.

Even though teaching is essentially a solitary activity, in the sense that each teacher is faced with his or her own responsibilities and professional duties, teamwork is essential, particularly at the secondary level, in order to improve the quality of education and adapt it more closely to the special characteristics of classes or groups of pupils.

The Commission stresses the importance of exchanges of teachers and partnerships between institutions in different countries. As is confirmed by current activities, such exchanges and partnerships provide an essential added value not only for the quality of education but also for a greater receptivity to other cultures, civilizations and experiences.

All these lines of emphasis should be the subject of a dialogue, or even of contracts, with teachers' organizations which go beyond the purely corporatist nature of such forms of collaboration; over and above their aims of defending the moral and material interest to their members, teachers' organizations have built up a fund of experience which they are willing to make available to policy makers.

8. Choices for Education : The Political Factor

Choosing a type of education means choosing a type of society. In all countries, such choices call for extensive public debate, based on an accurate evaluation of education systems. The Commission invites the political authorities to encourage such debate, in order to reach a democratic consensus, this being the best route to success for educational reform strategies.

The Commission advocates the implementation of measures for involving the different persons and institutions active in society in educational decision-making: administrative decentralization and the autonomy of educational establishments are conducive in most cases, it believes, to the development and generalization of innovation.

In view of the foregoing, the Commission wishes to reaffirm the role of the political authority, which has the duty clearly to define options and ensure overall regulation, making the required adjustments: education is a community asset which cannot be regulated by market forces alone.

The Commission none the less does not underrate the force of financial constraints and it advocates the bringing into operation of public/private partnerships. In developing countries, the public funding of basic education remains a priority, but the choices made must not imperil the coherence of the system as a whole, nor lead to other levels of education being sacrificed.

It is essential that funding structures be reviewed in the light of the principle that learning should continue throughout individuals' lives. The Commission hence feels that the proposed study-time entitlement, as briefly outlined in the report, deserves to be discussed and explored.

The progress of the new information and communication technologies should give rise to a general deliberation on access to knowledge in the world of tomorrow. The Commission recommends :

- the diversification and improvement of distance education through the use of the new technologies :
- greater use of those technologies in adult education and especially in the in-service training of teachers :
- the strengthening of developing countries' infrastructures and capabilities in this field and the dissemination of such technologies throughout society; these are in any case prerequisites to their use in formal education systems: and
- the launching of programmes for the dissemination of the new technologies under the auspices of UNESCO.

9. International Cooperation : Educating the Global Village

The need for international co-operation - which itself has to be radically rethought - is felt also in the field of education. This is an issue not only for education policy makers and the teaching profession but for all who play an active part in community life.

At the level of international co-operation, a policy of strong encouragement for the education of girls and women should be promoted, in the spirit of the Beijing Conference.

So-called aid policy should be made to evolve towards partnership by fostering, among other things, co-operation and exchanges within regional groupings.

A quarter of development aid should be devoted to the funding of education.

Debt swaps should be encouraged in order to offset the adverse effect of adjustment policies and policies for the reduction of domestic and foreign deficits on educational spending.

National education systems should be helped to gain strength by encouraging alliances and co-operation between ministries at regional level and between countries facing similar problems.

Countries should be helped to stress the international dimension of the education provided (curricula, use of information technologies and international co-operation).

New Partnerships between international institutions dealing with education should be encouraged through, for example, the launching of an international project for disseminating and implementing the concept of learning throughout life, on the lines of the inter-agency initiative that resulted in the Jomtien Conference.

The gathering, at international level, of data on national investment in education should be encouraged, in particular by the establishment of suitable indicators: total amount of private funds, investment by industry, spending on non-formal education, etc.

A set of indicators should be developed for revealing the most serious dysfunctions of education systems, by cross-relating various quantitative and qualitative data, such as : level of spending on education, drop-out rates, disparities in access, inefficiency of different parts of this system, poor-quality teaching, teachers' status, etc.

With an eye to the future, a UNESCO observatory should be set up to look into the new information technologies, their evolution and their foreseeable impact on not only education systems but also on modern societies.

Intellectual co-operation in the field of education

should be encouraged through the intermediary of UNESCO : UNESCO professorships. Associated Schools, equitable sharing of knowledge between countries, dissemination of information technologies, and student teacher and researcher exchanges.

UNESCO's normative action on behalf of Member States, for instance in relation to the harmonization of national legislation with international instruments, should be intensified.

***

Members of the Commission

Formally established at the beginning of 1993, the International Commission on Education for the Twenty First Century developed its Report over eight plenary and eight working group sessions held around the world. Chaired by Jacques Delors (France), Former president of the European Commission, its 14 members are as follows : In 'am Al-Mufti (Jordan), specialist on the status of women; Isao Amagi (Japan), educator, special adviser to the Minister of Education, Science and Culture; Roberta Carneiro (Portugal), president of TVI (Televisao Independente); Fay Chung (Zimbabwe), former Minister of Education; Bronislaw Geremek (Poland), historian, Member of Parliament; William Gorham (USA), specialist in public policy; Aleksandra Kornhauser (Slovenia), director of the International Centre for Chemical Studies; Michael Manley (Jamaica), former Prime Minister; Marisela Padron Quera (Venezuela), sociologist, former Minister of the Family; Marie-Angelique Savane (Senegal), sociologist; Karan Singh (India), diplomat and several times minister; Rodolfo Stavenhagen (Mexico), researcher in political and social scinece; Myong Won Suhr (Republic of Korea), former Minister of Education; Zhou Nanzhao (China), educator, professor at the China National Institute for Educational Studies

*(for full text of the report order —**Learning : The Treasure Within**, ISBN 92 3-103274-7, US $ 30.00 + 6.00; UNESCO Publishing, Paris, France)*

5

'Learning to be' in Retrospect

—*Asher Deleon*

Almost a quarter of a century ago, UNESCO published the findings of a world enquiry into education in a report entitled '**Learning to Be**'. *How does this landmark study look today?*

In 1972, the International Commission on the Development of Education chaired by the former French prime minister Edgar Faure published a report entitled *Learning to Be.* The title reflected the climate of euphoria and optimism of the times, generated by economic and social achievements, the ideology of steady progress, the official process of decolonialization then being completed, the positive consequences of "peaceful coexistence", and an enduring faith in international co-operation. It is true that student revolt and the "events" of 1968 had revealed a certain disenchantment, but the Report was based on data from the previous decade. The first signs of what later came to be regarded as an "education crisis" were just beginning to appear.

The Key Ideas

"Lifelong education" and "the learning society" were the Report`s two key ideas. The former was considered as the "keystone" of educational policies; the latter as a strategy aimed at committing society as a whole to education. The approach was based on the idea of osmosis between education and society, and sought to steer clear of a number of misconceptions such as the ideas of education as a "sub-system" of society, of instruction as a tool for solving all individual and social problems, and of the compartmentalization of life into "learning time" and "time for living".

As its title indicates, the Report focuses on learning, a process that goes beyond education and, *a fortiori*, teaching. Education and teaching are described in it as dimensions that are subordinate to the learning process. School and out-of-school activities (formal, non-formal and informal education) are treated without hierarchical distinction, and the importance of basic education for all and of adult education is taken as a premise : "learning is a process that lasts a lifetime, both in its duration and in its diversity."

However, the Commission did not regard lifelong education as a process of permanent schooling, adult education or continuous vocational training. It was seen neither as an educational system nor an educational field, but rather as "a principle on which the overall organization of a system and hence the elaboration of each of its parts, are based". Lifelong education is a need that is common to everyone.

Learning must be redistributed not only in time, but also in space. Thus the Faure Commission called into question the monopoly of institutionalized education. All institutions, whatever their field of competence (economic, social, cultural or informational) can be used for educational purposes and thereby help to build "a self-aware learning society".

The Report focused on personal development and put learners, not teachers or educational institutions, at the core of education. The important thing is not the path followed by the learner, but the outcome of the learning process. Each one of us must be free, as our judgment grows stronger and our experience becomes richer and more varied, to choose the ways best suited to our own needs, expectations and abilities.

The Education Gap

Starting from these basic concepts, the Commission put forward a series of suggestions and proposals for a new organization of education systems designed to do away with antiquated or unjustified barriers and to rid traditional structures of their excessively formal nature.

I am convinced that the basic ideas of the Faure Report are still relevant in the final decade of the twentieth century and that from their standpoint the education gap—the backwardness, dysfunctions and shortcoming of education in relation to human needs—can gradually the overcome. The theory behind these general guidelines is virtually never contested nowadays. Thousands of experiments in recent decades have been carried out along these lines. At the same time, a battle still has to be waged against conservatism at national level, the inadequate commitment of international organizations, external interference in the domestic affairs of many states, and the rigidity of administrative, productive and other structures, including the teaching profession.

Only a few countries (including Canada, Japan, Sweden, Norway and Argentine) have taken their cue from the Faure Report's suggestions at the national level. Most experiments, although frequently interesting and bold, carried out by local authorities, business firms, educational establishments and associations have been fragmentary and sporadic, with limited resources. Even countries that have long-established democratic and educational traditions and achievements as well as substantial financial resources hesitate to stray from the beaten track and integrate changes in the overall context.

Utopian Leanings

One criticism that could be made of *Learning to Be* is that it expected too much of education and did not take sufficient account of economic and political conditions. It also overestimated the material resources of the developing countries and the extent to which the industrialized countries were really willing to provide them with substantial aid. The by-passing of religious phenomena and their impact on education and the over looking of the ever widening education gap between individuals, and between ethnic groups, social classes and nations also reflect a lack of realism that has given rise to disappointments.

The results achieved in the different branches of education are far from satisfactory. The tiny percentage of young children enrolled in pre-school education (a percentage that is declining in several countries), the enormous numbers of children who receive no schooling at all, the figure of one billion illiterates by the end of the century, and the almost universal erosion of adult education—these are facts that make it imperative to radically revise objectives and strategic forecasts in these fields. Although the primary responsibility lies with the national and local authorities, the responsibility of the international community, and particularly that of UNESCO, should not be minimized. Indeed, it might well be asked how far and with what success UNESCO communicated the message of the Report.

New Parameters

Clearly, at the end of the 1960s it was impossible to predict the collapse of the Berlin Wall and the failure of the communist experiment, and the Faure Commission did not have the means to study the issues connected with the problems of indoctrination, education subject to censorship, and manipulation of and by education. However, the speed with which political regimes have collapsed, the slow progress of the necessary reforms, the domestic conflicts, both political and armed, inter ethnic and religious, and the subjective obstacles to the establishment of a market economy cannot be understood without reference to the distortions suffered by educational practices in previous decades. The International Commission on Education for the Twenty-First Century chaired by Jacques Delors may fill this gap, especially since the international climate is favourable to it. The failure of totalitarian regimes has encouraged the growing ascendancy of the philosophy of human rights, and it is increasingly clear that it is in the link between education and democracy or, better still, between education and freedom, that we should seek the guiding principle of our educational policies.

In the field of economics, the Faure Commission was able to benefit from the auspicious situation created after three decades of post war efforts and the first two decades of diagonalization. The Delors Commission has had to confront a far gloomier and more disturbing economic picture : crisis affecting the South, the debt burden, the collapse of terms of trade for the main raw materials, the ever-widening gap between industrialized and developing countries (with the exception of a few Asian countries at an intermediate stage of development), unemployment, the social and economic marginalization of a section of the urban and rural populations in the industrialized countries.

Another question concerns the role of the state. Disenchantment about the principle of total, and even sometimes partial, state control over education, budget austerity and the gulf between educational supply and demand, as well as danger arising from the "commercialization" of education, have sometimes led to questioning of the role of the state as the sole manager of education and its main source of funding. Some have suggested that it should become a mere regulator, responsible for maintaining an equitable system for distributing resources and enforcing national standards for examinations and qualifications. Others go even further. The Delors Commission was bound to take these problems into account.

The changes that have occurred in the educational sciences in the last quarter of a century are so far reaching that they can be called revolutionary. The Faure Commission saw the new educational technologies as a prerequisite for bringing about most of the innovations. Today, however, after the explosion of computer technology, multimedia and interactive systems, the Delors Commission has had to pay great attention to what Henri Dieuzeide, a French authority in this field, has called “a new visual order”. “The audiovisual media present, information technology organizes, telecommunications brings closer,” he notes in *Les Nouvelles Technologies, Outils d'Enseignement* (UNESCO/Nathan, Paris, 1994). “What is going to happen when any educational activity or exercise can be undertaken on a single piece of hardware containing messages that in the past were transmitted by an array of different media?... The result will be to force different and frequently antagonistic educational approaches to draw closer together and to work out common strategies for purposes of presentation, structuring and manipulation.”

Finally, humankind has entered a phase of historical transition marked by the conflict between human activities and environmental constraints. We must invent a new paradigm of development geared to the concept of sustainability and define the ethical rules pertaining to it. We have no choice but to build up new modes of production and consumption. Far from being masters of the universe, we must understand that we are but the guests or stewards of nature. It is through education that we must “learn to be” nature's partner and co-pilot.

— Asher Deleon

Executive Secretary of the International Commission on the Development of Education (1972) which produced the “Learning to Be” report.

(Source : The UNESCO Courier, April 1996)

6

Opening New Doors in Science Education

— *Francois Gros*

In the twenty-first century, humanity will have an opportunity to achieve an ambition that his moral as well as technical implications : it will be able to attain an all encompassing view of planet earth. Modern communication technology, modern means of transport and satellite based observation are already bringing the various parts of the world closer together, and there are good grounds for believing that, as a result, there will be far fewer remaining pockets of political and cultural isolation.

The planet-wide view thus made possible by scientific and technological progress nonetheless raises a problem of principle, indeed almost a philosophical problem: unless a very lofty purpose is assigned to science, unless the science we produce is more than merely utilitarian, there will be no means of surmounting a major cultural conflict that we have seen developing at the end of this century, one that is in fact much more serious than in generally realized.

Decompartmentalizing Science

The benefits of science and technology no longer seem so obvious as they did in the last century. Before the major conflicts of our own times, science was expected to solve most of humankind's individual and general problems.

War has demonstrated that science has not succeeded in changing mentalities and that barbarism still lurks beneath the surface of civilization. Current debates over environmental issues and bioethics also reflect a certain "culture gap" between science and society. The ecological movement has not only put science in an awkward position, it has put it on trail. In order to overcome the disenchantment now felt towards it, science needs to be set within a far wider cultural context.

One of the main dangers threatening science teaching comes from overspecialization. Although specialization is undoubtedly a necessary condition for the improved training of engineers and technicians, overspecialization is in danger of alienating science from the general public because it makes communication more difficult and raises a serious problem of social "acceptability". It is already becoming evident, for instance, that research in biology is likely to be held back more by ethical and cultural considerations than by economic ones.

Overspecialization may also lead to a lack of "culture". Scientists must learn to respect and practise other forms of language and communication, while conversely, it would be extremely dangerous to reject science on the pretext of getting back to humanitarian values. *Science is part and parcel of culture*, and the practice of science should lead naturally tolerance.

Science teaching is at present in a rut and needs to be re-examined. This applies particularly to textbooks. Physics is taught from books on physics, and biology from works on biology, whereas science teaching should be much more cross-disciplinary. Why not refer to the underlying problems of physics when teaching molecular biology or, when teaching biology, to the ethical questions that are soon sure to come up?

The problem needs to be tackled both in general and in specific terms. Due regard must be shown both for the different cultures of different countries and for the universality of science. This is the only way to avoid fragmentation of knowledge, which is harmful in every way. Science education will also have to be integrated with other forms of education—literary , artistic, political or even economic—in order that the citizens of the twenty-first century may see science primarily as an ally in achieving what they want done for the good of their country or of civilization as a whole.

More Open, More Diverse Higher Education

After going through a period of crisis, in Europe especially, universities can now aspire to provide both a general culture and a practical training for various occupations. It is, however, increasingly true to say that the training of scientists cannot be confined to a single location.

First of all it will probably be necessary to rethink the transition from secondary education to higher education. The former sharp break between them is becoming less abrupt. Much still remains to be done, however, because in a way school students today are more mature than their predecessors. In my opinion they are far more receptive to science, technology and discussion about social problems than is generally believed.

They first go to university to learn the basics, then to laboratories to round out what they have learned, then into industry to study the technical applications, and in some cases to museums or science parks to acquire a broader overall view of science. This form of networking, linking the university with other professional institutions, will need to be reinforced in the future. Perhaps we should also rethink and diversify the traditional linear progression from school to university, laboratory or business.

Furthermore, universities should not all necessarily teach the same thing nor attempt to cover all the ground. Although a common core must be established, i.e. a basic scientific culture without which studies cannot be carried forward, universities nevertheless have to find their own specific roles in keeping with the aspirations of the societies (and regions) within which they operate. The evaluation of universities should, however, be carried out at international level: while cultural traditions and national goals vary from country to country, science is preeminently universal in character.

The growth of the student population in universities raises considerable problems, since it necessitates the training of adequate numbers of specialist teachers in various fields. Universities should therefore have an open-door policy and should allow scientists great freedom of movement, both within their own country and internationally. Although this means that they should set their sights high and have plentiful resources, they cannot restrict themselves to training an elite. The French "Grandes Ecoles", for instance, provide an excellent education and produce some remarkable people, but perhaps they fail to take account of the diversity of individual talents. The Grandes Ecoles, in my view to their credit, are making a real effort to open up to the wider university system and to the business world.

Thought should also be given to the possibly disproportionate importance attached to mathematics in the selection of students. Mathematics is one of the highest forms of intellectual activity and can be used to assess an individual's capacity for abstraction and rapid thinking, but it is going too far to take it as the sole criterion.

Teaching Students to be Team Players

If we are looking for a system that is fully appropriate to the needs of the coming century and as receptive as possible to all forms of cultures, we need to prepare the ground in primary and secondary schools. By the university level it is already too late. I believe it is essential to introduce the teaching of the history of science from the primary level on, so as to situate science within a cultural context.

Science would then be gradually integrated into the teaching process in a pluralist way, with efforts being made to maintain a balance with other subjects and outlooks.

In secondary school, hands-on scientific experiments should be introduced at a very early stage. This is crucial, since such activities bring students face to face with their responsibilities, teaching them that they must be able to work as members of a team, must have an acutely critical outlook and must realize that there is not just one, but several possible approaches to the solution of problems—in short, that life itself puts us in situations that constantly require us to solve difficult practical problems.

There have long been calls for secondary-level science to be taught in this way, but it is not easy to set up. The logistics are expensive, and teachers are not always adequately trained for this kind of work. This is one of the reasons why France has established university-level teacher education institutes (Instituts Univesitaires de Formation de Maîtres), whose students have the opportunity to take training courses in laboratory work. The institutes aim to provide an inter-disciplinary training course, showing how problems are linked to one another, not only across subject boundaries but also within society as a whole, while enabling trainees from different backgrounds to establish a close relationship with experimental science. It is, however, too soon to pass judgment on the effectiveness of these institutions.

The acquisition of knowledge in the twenty-first century will probably be a halfway house between computerised messages of the highest level of abstraction at one end of the spectrum and highly specialized, sophisticated technologies at the other: scientists will therefore have to be able to move freely between these two extremes.

— Francois Gros

Permanent Secretary, French Academy of Science, France

(Source: The UNESCO Courier, April 1996)

7

Schools at the Crossroads

— *Robert Bisaillon*

The school must adapt to a world where it no longer has a monopoly on the transmission of knowledge

Schools often seem to be standing still while the rest of the world moves on. However, a number of social changes now look set to challenge educational systems, and the functions of education.

Schools are at a crossroads. On the one hand, the state seems unwilling to go on financial and directing education; on the other, schools and local authorities would like to have more of a say in these matters themselves.

In these circumstances, the role of schools and their place in society become less straightforward than they were. In competition with other institutions such as the family and the workplace, which are themselves in the throes of change, schools no longer have a monopoly on the dissemination of knowledge. New information and communication technologies are putting teachers to the test and making them re-examine their approach to education.

The ways by which young people acquire knowledge have changed. Acquisition by absorption, a process encouraged by the media, is taking over from the traditional process in which the family and the school acted as the intermediaries. But the media appeal to young people's curiosity and emotional responses in a random fashion, and schools find it very hard to put knowledge acquired from the media into some sort of order so that school children can benefit from it.

The concept of skills has also taken on a broader meaning. As well as transmitting knowledge and know-how to their pupils, teachers must train them to find information for themselves and to make use of it. Pupils' skills are now defined in terms of their self reliance and their ability to adapt to different types of training and jobs.

In a society where there is more and more cultural intermingling and where there are fewer and fewer fixed points of reference, teachers are expected to show children how to form their own values.

Lastly, the phenomenon of students "working their way through college" is a typical feature of life in North America, where the school population is drawn from mixed, multiethnic backgrounds. All these factors have a strong influence on thinking about what is required of schools and about ways of achieving integration.

Education and Politics

The situation raises a number of socio-political questions, such as how to reconcile elitism with democracy without widening social cleavages or how to expound a universal culture respectful of national identities without encouraging racism and intolerance.

In this context, how should the roles of the state, the school and the individual be defined? A definition of a "common public culture", encompassing a set of non-negotiable values that are necessary to social cohesion, is perhaps called for. This set of values could serve as a common core for the education of all groups, minority or majority, sedentary or nomadic, without infringing the basic rights of any of them. These consensual values could justifiably be invoked to challenge the authority of schools designed to emphasize religious or ethnic differences. Again, instead of introducing new subjects into syllabuses, would it not be better to reorganize existing syllabuses transversally to encourage knowledge and understanding of other languages and cultures? Education could in this way become truly a factor working for peace.

On a matter more directly related to the social and economic context, the kind of general knowledge that opens pupils' minds to the world around them needs to be combined with vocational qualifications enabling them to find a place in economic life. Since one of the aims of education is to provide young people with the means of changing the society in which they live, they should first understand how it works and how it can be improved.

In all these respects teachers have a leading role to play, which is why one of the most basic changes to the system concerns the teaching profession. More emphasis in pre-service training should be attached to teachers' individual and collective responsibility, i.e. the development of professionalism should be the guiding principle. Next, in view of the length of teachers' careers, pre-service training, practical experience and in-service training should form a continuum. Success depends on responsible commitment, by each according to his or her role and competence, on the part of all those who determine educational policies, who are in charge of schools and whose daily business in education.

— Robert Bisaillon

President, Education Board of Governors, Canada

(Source : The UNESCO Courier, April 1996)

8

Globalization of Education : Roles and Barriers

— L. Gien, J. Malpas & G. Skanes

Introduction

It has been well recognized that economic development depends largely on the level of education and training of the workforce. In the twenty-first century, with increased global migration and global trading, education must be globalized to facilitate optimum communication and contribution of people to the global economy.

Internationalization of education involves, in part, true exchange of personnel and technologies among countries. This exchange allows first hand experience and deeper understanding of other cultures, their values, and approaches, which promote more tolerance, respect and appreciation of cultural differences. To a certain extent, the exchange of personnel and technologies have been occurring . It has been, however, a true equal two-way exchange, since more students and faculty from the developing countries study and work in the developed nations and less vice versa. This tends to promote the values of developed countries perhaps inappropriately at times, and hinder a full understanding of the cultures of developing countries and their environments. On behalf of Canadian Students and educators, we must promote an increased participation of

Canadians in the educational establishments and in training programs of the developing country.

The true exchange of information, education may have been impeded by barriers such as level of literacy, unequal share of resources among countries including technology, communication facilities and current differences in the organization of education systems.

To prepare individuals and societies for the global economy of the twenty-first century, education must erase the barriers preventing true exchange of experience/information mentioned above. To achieve this purpose, education should:

- Increase the level of literacy of the world population so that all people can read, understand and use their own language.
- expose students to other cultures, values to promote cross cultural understanding and tolerance of cultural differences. This may be done by requiring that part of the educational program be completed in another country.
- foster the formation of international guidelines/standards for various occupations and educational milestones to facilitate recognition of educational qualifications and working experiences of people who have moved their place of origin to contribute to other countries.
- foster research linkage and collaboration among interdisciplinary teams of various regions of the World.
- emphasize lifelong, continuing learning to prepare workers for rapid changes in knowledge and technologies.
- promote critical thinking and adaptability to facilitate adaptation to a quick changing society.
- formulate an international language for technologies.

Conclusion

In summary, globalization of education is a necessity to prepare individuals and societies for the next century when global enterprises, true partnerships and global migration will be prominent features.

Dr Lan Gien
Dr John Malpas
Dr. Graham Skanes
Memorial University of Newfoundland
St. John's N.F.,
Canada A1C 5S7

(Source: International Commission for the Twenty-First Century)

9

Education, Social Change and Development: Education Level Effects on Fertility and Child Health/Mortality

— *Mouna L. Samman*

Introduction

During the last twenty years, much attention has been focused on studying the effects of education on fertility and mortality, this subject being englobed within a more general theme of relationships among education, social change and development. From the large amount of accumulated research to date on the topic, it is observed that the impact of female education on fertility, child health and mortality is stronger than either that of male education or any other household characteristic. It seems that education, measured by length of attendance to school, sets off important changes in Women's situations in ways which in turn impinge directly or indirectly on fertile and mortality. Source of Knowledge and means for exposure to modern life, education is also recognized as an important factor for women's empowerment, enabling them to acquire more autonomy in decision-making and greater control over material resources.

Although it is widely recognized that the enhancement of women's education is critical for fertility reduction, a country needs to achieve a particular level of development before a negative effect of education can be observed on fertility : in early stages of development, lower or upper primary education can increase, or at best have a negligible effect on fertility. Moreover, it was observed in diverse societies, that there is a threshold level of education beyond which reductions in fertility are generated: most often at the level of some secondary schooling of approximately after seven to eight years of schooling.

Education has the potential to both increase fertility and reduce it in at least three quite unintentional ways. In delay in entry into marriage, education shortens the overall length of time during which a women is exposed to the risk of pregnancy. Furthermore, education has frequently been observed to provoke decline in the duration and intensity of breast feeding and in postpartum abstinence among more educated women, thus resulting in an increase in fertility. Finally, education is associated with improved child survival, which implies longer birth intervals and therefore a slower pace of childbearing. The strength of these opposing effects varies considerably depending on the cultural and developing contexts.

Through studies we have evidence that, at early stages of development, the primary effect of education is through inadvertent fertility enhancing factors; thereafter through delayed marriage, an inadvertent but fertility depressing factor; this effect gradually weakens and is probably overtaken by the effects trough deliberate demand-related factors. Parental demands for children are influenced, as well, by the mother's education level. For example, important motives dictation family size desires include the strength of the son preference. The evidence is that this preference is eroded only after a relatively high level of education has been achieved. Another motive underlying family size desires concerns the extent of women's dependence on reproduction for social acceptance - namely children as a source of prestige - and on children, or sons, for economic security. It is when economic realities for women become more secure and their and their relative power in household decision-making more comprehensive, that the effect of education through a lower desired family size and increased contraception become important for fertility. The stage at which this occurs depends largely on the cultural context; it is conditioned by the position that women occupy in the traditional kinship structure of a society.

The process through which women's education influences child nutritional/health conditions and mortality is more direct and less complex than for fertility. Recent studies, covering countries in different stages of development, concluded that even a small amount of education affects child mortality levels, the impact being stronger from ages 1 to 4, than during the initial first year of life. It was also observed that educational attainment of the mothers may also reduce spontaneous foetal deaths and have relationships with the low weight of babies at birth. Maternal education increases women's knowledge about health and diseases and awareness of beneficial hygienic and nutritional practices; it promotes utilization of existing health services and facilities. Improved urban structures and expanded efficient health care systems actually contribute to morbidity and mortality gains.

Conclusion

That schooling has a powerful and pervasive effect on reproductive behaviour, child health and mortality is undisputed. The content of the school curriculum - particularly when focussing on issues related to population, health and reproductive life - the organization of instruction and the social process of learning, are of utmost importance as well. In this framework, basic education for all is a prerequisite and the minimum level to attain for any sustainable strategy addressing population concerns. Accumulated evidence provides a compelling rationale for advocating increased investment in education and the elimination of institutional and cultural barriers to women's access to schooling. From a policy point of view, it is more important to note however that a higher level of education is still needed for girls to change their orientation toward life and more specifically toward reproductive family life. It is therefore necessary to envisage expanding the opportunities for secondary education and training, especially for girls.

Further Reading

Bicego, George T; Ties Boerma, J. *Maternal Education and Child Survival: a Comparative Analysis of DHS Data.* Demographic and Health Surveys World Conference, Washington D.C., 5-7 August 1991, Vol. 1, 1991.

Cochrane, Susan H. *Fertility and Education: What Do We Really Know?* Baltimore, John Hopkins University Press, 1979.

Cochrane, Susan H.; and Samir, M. Farid. Fertility *in Sub-Saharan Africa: Analysis and Explanation.* Washington D.C., The World Bank, (World Bank Discussion Papers 43), 1989.

Jejeebhoy, Shireen. *Women's Education, Fertility and the Proximate Determinants of Fertility,* presented at the Expert Group Meeting on population and Women, Gaborone, 22-26 June 1992.

United Nations. *Fertility Behaviour in the Context of Development: Evidence from the World Fertility Survey.* New York, United Nations, 1987.

United Nations. *Population and Women : A Review of Issues and Trends.* New York, United Nations, 1992, (Background paper, presented by the United Nations Secretariat at the Expert Group Meeting on Population and Women - preparatory to the International Conference on Population and Development, Cairo 1994 - Gaborone, 22-26 June 1992.)

Ms Mouna L. Samman
Programme Specialist
Environment and Population Education and
Information for Human Development (ED/EDP)
UNESCO
Paris, France

(Source: International Commission on Education for the Twenty First Century)

10

The Learning Society and Development

— *Guy Bessette*

Introduction

In today's information society, the educational and social view of the school and of the educational process is still linked to the educational paradigm of the industrial society. That paradigm defined educational needs and conditions in terms of access to knowledge, the initial training of the labour force and the choice of the school as a medium for education and learning. On the threshold of the year 2000, however, these needs and conditions are no longer the same and call less for reform than for a redefinition of the educational paradigm. This redefinition should take into account not only social and technological changes in global society but also the development needs of the countries of the South.

1. **Access to Education :** In most developing countries, the traditional education system is no longer able to meet the needs created by the geographical explosion or offer access to education as a factor of social equality. This raises the issue of the quality, still very poor in a number of countries, which could cancel out the advances made in quantitate terms (Vespoor, 1989). The challenge is therefore is to offer access to education while improving its quality in a context of scarcity not only of financial and material

resources but also of human resources. New approaches to the development of education are needed. The present "More of the same" approach makes the problem worse instead of helping to solve it.

2. Training of the Labour Force : Nowadays, education can no longer be considered as an initial stage in the training of the labour force. Firstly, rapid technological change requires the continual updating of knowledge and know-how, i.e. continuing or lifelong training, and schools are no longer able to keep pace with technological, social and economic developments. Indeed, we are seeing the development of parallel vocational training systems alongside the traditional educational system. We are therefore called on to redefine the educational process so that stress is no longer placed on quickly outmoded contents but on the capacity to learn and think, to search for, organize and structure relevant information and to develop necessary skills.

Secondly, the school's inability to meet labour market needs aggravates the economic crisis. Unemployed school-leavers, who cannot find a place on the labour market, and young people who dropped out of school largely because of its irrelevance to the labour market, widen the gap between rich and poor, intensifying social pressure. This means that education is holding development back rather than encouraging it.

Lastly, the needs of present-day society cannot be confined to making its members more technically competent: they involve the all-round development of the individual. They make us realize the importance of education in its practical application as a process for the development of individuals' potential so that they can improve their own well-being and that of the society in which they live.

3. Venus and Techniques for Accessing Knowledge : Television, computers, data telecommunication and several other information technologies now offer a multitude of ways of obtaining knowledge outside the school framework. It has even been suggested in this connection that the communication society is transforming itself into a learning society (Serres, 1991). The teaching methods and techniques of the communication media and distance education makes it possible to expand both teaching resources and the capacity to access education while making available a greater number of good quality teaching aids. In so doing, they provide answers to the problem of the quality of teaching, to that of the quality of the conditions for learning and, lastly, to the imperative need to broaden access to education, Finally, the swiftness with which the contents to which they give access are created, processed and modified helps to reduce the timelag between the world of education and the world of work.

But we should not expect it to solve all our problems. Despite very promising applications in both formal and non-formal education, the great expectations held out for distance education as high-quality, cost-effective means of providing education for all are far from having been met (Arger, 1990; Hawkridge, 1988).

It is also important to stress that recourse to new channels must not be merely the mediatized extension of an education based on the transmission of information and contents. Active learner involvement is fundamental since it is the learner who constructs his/her knowledge on the basis of this information and content. It is therefore not enough to make learning more "technological". We should redefine educational needs, the ways in which our response to them can be organized and the learning process within educational practice. We have to go beyond the concept of knowledge as something that is transmitted and consumed, and of the school as a machine to transmit of knowledge of facility of learning.

Lastly, it is important to focus the assimilation of educational contents on learners' need and not on the traditional segmentation of subject matter. New information and communication technologies allow a distinction to be drawn between the gathering of information and learning experience, enabling the latter to focus on learners' needs (taking into consideration their social, economic, cultural and cognitive profile) and defining the role of the teacher as facilitator in this process.

Conclusion

Today, there are 300 million children who still do not attend either primary or secondary school and more than a thousand million adults are still illiterate (UNDP, 1991). To this number, additional millions have to be added who only have access to very poor quality education and all those who drop out of the educational system and who go on to swell the ranks of those deprived of access to both knowledge and work. The World Conference on Education for All (Jomtien, Thailand, 1990), which considered basic education to be the priority action to develop education, introduced a key concept, that of catering to basic education needs in strategies designed to improve education. To give this concept practical application, we shall have to re-examine not only aims, curricular contents and teaching methods but also the educational paradigm inherited from another era, perpetuated by our education systems that have run out of steam and are now in crisis.

To do this, we believe that it is essential to give absolute priority to operational research on the learning society. The research agenda must focus on the use of different channels of communication placing emphasis on the learning process and not on the transmission of contents. Its aim would be to generate strategies to meet basic educational needs and direct education policies and approaches to that end. However, it can only be prepared and implemented through the worldwide consultation and co-ordination of the bodies and institutions that could make a contribution. We therefore ask UNESCO to launch an appeal for those worldwide consultation and co-ordination and to support the preparation and introduction of the research agenda for the learning society and development.

Further Reading

Arger, G., Distance education in the third world; critical analysis on the promise and reality, Open learning June 1990: 9-18.

Hawkridge, D., distance education and the World Bank, British journal of educational technology, vol. 19, #2, 1988 : 84-95.

Serres, M., Tiers-instruit, Paris, editions Francois Bourin, 1991.

UNDP, Human Development Report, Oxford University Press, 1991.

Vespoor, A., Pathways to change, improving the quality of education in developing countries, Washington, World Bank, 1989.

Young, M., Perraton, H., Jenkins, J., Doods, T., Distance teaching for the Third World, Cambridge, International Extension College, Second edition, 1991.

Mr Guy Bessette
Administrateur principal du programme
Centre de recherches pour le developpment
international (CRDI)
250, rue Albert - BP 8500
Ottawa (Ontario) Canada K1G 3HB

(Source: International Commission on Education for Twenty-First Century)

11

Developing New Models for a Learning Culture and Sustainable Learning Communities

— *Ian Morrison*

Introduction

We need a compatible and mutually reinforcing balance between a strong civil and an efficient economy.

The collapse of the economic base in many communities threatens the future of those communities. Adult learners are in crisis.

Learning is the key to managing in a future full of uncertainty.

We must create a lifelong learning culture which breaks the lockstep relationships of learning, earning, retiring.

We must re-invent structure that reinforce the essential links between being, becoming and belong.

Citizen empowerment and lifelong learning are fundamental ingredients of a learning society.

We need to restore a sense of collective responsibility, social justice and global stewardship as essential characteristics of good citizenship.

The public discourse on training and lifelong learning focuses too narrowly on job-related training. We risk limiting our efforts to a technocratic approach that has no lasting benefits and that only increases public skepticism.

A genuine learning culture includes public policies and structures which enable a meaningful role for citizens in the economic, political, social and cultural life of the community.

Citizen's groups and policy makers need to work together to define the essential characteristics (social, economic, cultural) of a learning society.

A learning culture recognizes that citizens have the wisdom and ability to address the problems confronting their community. It provides them with a measure of control over their participation, especially those who have been marginalized such as unemployed youth, older people, learning disadvantaged and minority groups.

A learning culture values creativity, sustainability, autonomy, self-directedness, individual and social responsibility, participation, and a capacity to care for the well-being of the community as a whole.

A learning society provides positive support for people during life transitions, e,g, learning, child care, job change, elder care, and retirement, if necessary.

We need to translate the rhetoric of "lifelong learning" into measurable socio-economic indicators of a learning society.

Research projects are required to develop instruments and methodology for measuring performance.

Innovative models of learning communities should be identified and tested for their sustainability.

Successful models should be highlighted and generic materials made available to support replication of such models in other places.

We recommend sustained multi-sector consultation on the nature of a learning culture.

We recommend support for research programs to identify indicators and tools for measurement of a learning society.

We recommend a plan to identity, test and replicate successful models of learning communities.

Mr Ian Morrison
Executive Director
Canadian Association for Adult Education
Corbett House
29 Prince Arthur Avenue
Toronto (Ontario) M5R 1B2, Canada

(Source: International Commission on Education for the Twenty First Century)

12

Education For Freedom And Social Responsibility: The Rudolf Steiner Schools (Waldorf Pedagogy)

— Sigrid Niedermayer-Tahri

"In school the question is not of receiving a complete education, but rather of preparing oneself to receive it from life". (R.Steiner)

Steiner Schools try to advocate a new spirit in a rapidly changing world; a purely materialistic conception of the world and of the human being is no longer sufficient to respond to questions posed in our industrial society. The future requires a fundamental change in our way of thinking: the human individual as an independent spiritual entity should be the starting point for all efforts aiming at the renewal of our society. Based on a profound knowledge of human nature, the principles of the pedagogy of Rudolf Steiner (also called Waldorf pedagogy) can be summarized as follows:

- **All human faculties - intellectual, artistic, moral** - are developed in an equal manner. The curriculum of each school is individually devised, and there is always a balance between theory and practice. Arts and science subjects are given equal importance. At secondary school level, practical courses on agriculture, forestry, surveying, and internships in industrial and social environments are included in the curriculum.

- **Teaching** is considered and practised as an art. The teachers act like artists whose aims are to help the child to discover and love the world surrounding him or her. Their aim is not to cram the child with knowledge, but to awaken at the right moment certain faculties of the soul, of the inner self. In everyday practice the question is not "what is possible?" or "what goes down well?" but rather "what is challenging and what may best stimulate the pupil at the present state of development?" Therefore children stay together in age groups; there is no selection or early specialization and know repetition. The diversity in every class reflects the diversity of humanity as a fundamental basis for social education. This philosophy is in keeping with the 1966 ILO-UNESCO Recommendation on the status of teachers (in particular provision III).

- The teacher's roles are to **awaken** the child's **latent faculties** and allow its **profound individuality** to emerge and develop: they thus help the children to find the appropriate relation between their individuality and physical being, their environment and the present-day society into which they are to integrate. It is this relation which enable them to make the appropriate use of their freedom. Young people are then enable to enter into society not as passive spectators, but as conscious sensitive citizens, ready to tackle the challenges of our times by taking an active part in the transformation of our world.

Organisation and Management of the School

Steiner School are self-governing and have no school head or director, but are run by the teachers, who all have equal rights and decide on all administrative matters (teaching concept, employment of teachers, buildings, finances, etc.). Based on mutual trust and comprehension, the bonds between parents and teachers are cultivated through frequent meetings. Parents also participate in important decisions and take on an active part in school life. This sets an example of democracy to the pupils.

Steiner Schools are private schools, financed partially by the state or the local community, as well as by parents who contribute in a spirit of mutual aid, enabling low-income families to enrol their children also.

In 1993 there exist, worldwide, over 600 Rudolf Steiner schools, 1000 kindergartens, and 500 institutions or remedial education and social therapy. Some Steiner schools are members of the international network of UNESCO's Associated Schools Project.

In France, Steiner Schools can be visited at the Federation des Ecoles Steiner en France, 5, rue Georges Clemenceau 78400 Chatou, France, telephone no. (33-1) 3952 6917.

Education in Critical Environments

The originality of this educational approach and its longstanding practical application all over the world have recently proved to be particularly interesting and fruitful in such disadvantaged environments as slums, refugee camps or in conflicts situations, conditions where alternative channels of education often prove to be more efficient than official school systems. The following pilot projects are outstanding examples of the success of this alternative method and they might be of great benefit to other situations and countries :

- Soweto and Alexandra (South Africa) : schools in various black townships :
- Shati refugee camp (Gaza strip) : Kindergarten and remedial education for Palestinian children ;
- Zagreb (Croatia); Kindergarten;
- Favela Monte Azul, Sao Paolo (Brazil) : schooling and

work with marginal groups and street children using the principles of steiner education;

- Holywood, Belfast (Northern Ireland) : Protestant and Catholic children are taught together;
- Pine Ridge Reservation, South Dakota (U.S.A.): school for Sioux Indian children.

Further Reading

Carlgren, F. Eduquer vers la liberté, La pédagogie de Rudolf Steiner dans le mouvement international des écoles Waldorf, Les Trois Arches, Paris, 1992.

Craemer, U. Die favela-Kinder, Sozialarbeit am Rande der Gesellschaft, Stuttgart, 1987.

Edmunds, F. Rudolf Steiner Education, the Waldorf Schools, R. Steiner Press, London, 1992.

Geraets, T. Stars and Rainbows over Alexandra, Heidenheim, 1990.

Kiersch, J. Die Waldorfpädagogik, Eine Einfuhrung in die Pädagogik Rudolf Steiners, Stuttgart, 1992.

Krampen, I. Self governed Schools, Case Studies, E. Fuchs (ed.), Frankfurt, 1992.

Steiner, R. L'art de l'éducation, Méthode et pratique, (conférences), Triades, Paris, 1993. (Specialized bookstore : Pentagram', 15 rue Racine, 75006 Paris)

Ms. Sigrid Niedermayer - Tahri
Assistant Programme Specialist
Section for Humanistic, Cultural and International Education
UNESCO
75352 Paris 075P France

(Source: International Commission on Education for the Twenty First Century)

13

Process of Education : Role of the Worker/Learner

— *Wendy Terry*

Introduction

The process of education is changing as we adjust to a lifelong learning lifestyle and the role of the adult worker as learner needs to be considered within the context of these changes. While the role of "educational demand" was noted in the Commission Working Paper *Current Trends in Educational Reform*, it appears to limit its scope to parents and students. Adults and adult workers as learners, are key stakeholders in educational structures. It is well recognized that children and youth do better if their parents are educated; yet in developing educational policies we typically address only children's educational needs and ignore those of adults.

The worker's education movement was founded in the belief that workers should have democratic power over their learning. Adult/Worker educators believe that democratic learning processes are the most appropriate means of fostering adult learning in a democratic society. As the century nears its end, society is more interested in adults' educational attainment and gives more serious consideration to their learning needs because a more direct link has been identified between educational levels and economic prosperity.

Worker/Learners: Adult educators have made us aware that the nature of adult learner's participation differs from that of children, in part because adults are voluntary learners where children and youth are often compelled to attend school by law. However, many of the sociological aspects of adult education have not been examined and documented.

Between systems for adults and children, the social structure is different. One might describe children and youth education as a pyramid which you climb and for which there are rungs up: the academic plan. The academic plan is defined more by academics in the educational structure than by young learners.

For adults, the educational environment is more aptly demonstrated by a concentric ball diagram. The adult, at the centre, reaches out into various structures to catch what he or she can to meet his work-related, citizenship and personal learning needs. The workplace, social action groups, public libraries, media and the traditional pyramid of academic institutions are all resources for the worker/learner. The adult's academic plan is defined by the opportunities the learner has access to, rather than the educational structures themselves. Adults often use academic programmes in a way unintended by educational structures. One could take an Italian course not for "general interest" (an academic label), but because one is a nurse's aide in a nursing home with many Italian-speaking patients. What is not developed is an understanding of the learning paths of adults, creating a problematic information flaw.

Information : Adult learners need better information. The multiplicity of programme providers is a confusing maze. How does one know you have survived the lot? How can one link them together to meet one's needs? It is one thing to understand the various academic pyramids offered by public educational institutions, but it is an ordeal to understand how to knit together the learning opportunities from the variety of places within your reach.

The provision of information to adult users can be used to improve planning : if a business person wanted to plan better service, she might ask : What do we do? Who uses our services, and how? In adult education, these basic planning questions are rarely asked. The information is either not collected or is collected in an aberrant manner. For instance, adults are grouped into "full-time equivalents" as though their individual participation pattern did not count, only its equation to patterns characteristic of youth. Data bases which document what exists for adults also document what exists for planners. Documenting what adults are seeking and cannot find identifies the needs gap. Data collected by polling adults is needed to identify gaps. Information rooted in the true nature and needs of adults would improve the decision-making process for adults and planners.

While adults' needs cannot be identified via the model of adult learner as full-time equivalent, the needs of workers as learners are no better identified by business. While a business's worker training needs are important, the emerging labour markets require workers to be able to move from employer to employer and from one field of work to another. Planners need to ask the worker directly about his or her needs and workers now more than ever, need a direct role in decision-making.

Decision-Making : Due to the nature of their interaction with learning systems, adults use marketplace power more than children and youths. This marketplace power is being eroded due to a decline in discretionary spending power resulting from low waged or "jobless economies". This erosion is more common in developed countries where provision is often based in "user fees" than in developing countries where provision is more often provided by community, development or social action groups. Choices like "voucher systems" give consumers a wider range of choice, but they still leave the basic power to determine curriculum and methods in the hands of suppliers of providers. The worker's education movement believes that learners should be involved in all aspects of their learning.

Further Reading

Tedesco, Juan Carlos. *Current Trends in Educational Reform* (note prepared for the First Session of the International Commission on Education for the Twenty First Century), UNESCO, Paris, January 1993.

Ms Wendy Terry
International Federation of Worker's Educational Associations
736 Bathurst Street, Unit # 3
Toronto (Ontario), M5S 2R4 Canada

(Source: International Commission on Education for the Twenty First Century)

14

Education for Human Rights : Toward 2000 and Beyond

— *Maxwell Yalden*

Introduction

This brief will cover the first three "lines of inquiry": education and culture, education and citizenship and education and social cohesion. From the human rights perspective, all three are aspects of a single issue, which is summarized in the phrase "responsible participation in a pluralist society". One of the greatest dangers facing the international community in the twenty-first century will be growing public questioning of the ability of democratic societies to provide a fair measure of social justice to all. The promotion of pluralist principles has not been matched by effective changes in the social balance among groups. The educational problem is not to preach civic virtues to those who have benefited most but to persuade those who are marginalized that responsible participation serves their interests as well. In spite of - or perhaps because of - an unprecedented and accelerating intermingling of cultures, mutual tolerance will be at a premium. The tensions implicit in protecting cultural diversity while moderating its negative effects on social cohesion are common to many countries. The recent resurgence of petty nationalism and supremacist doctrines also suggests a deep-seated reluctance to subordinate ethnic loyalties in some overarching socio-political community. This brief proposes some educational approaches to take account of these phenomena.

It is contradictory to try to inculcate an appreciation of the values of diversity through educational systems that tend to be artificially stratified and vehicles of social dominance. In practice, the vaunted democratic equalities of standing and opportunity are very imperfectly and superficially realized. The message of "responsible participation in a pluralist society" must be better conveyed by the institutional characteristics of our education systems. The moral content lies in the medium itself. A totally "free market" in education is not consistent with equal access to equivalent educational opportunities, and we should not expect shared responsibility to emerge from unequal participation. Some of our efforts to provide socially integrated and culturally impartial education may have gone awry, but not all, and never entirely; the goal remains valid. With the explosion of information technologies, there is no reason—at least in developed societies - why young people should not have universal access to the very best teaching or a direct appreciation of pluralistic values within traditional classrooms settings. But schools and colleges will probably no longer be the most powerful formations influences in the development of social and life skills. We face a situation in which the power of parents and educators to screen or control what young people see, hear and do has declined. The process of transmitting our humanistic values must be necessity adapt to this very different world of social communications. Among the young, peer pressures are often paramount, and youth culture is easily captured by tribalistic and exclusive ideologies. These effects cannot be countered through mere academic or theoretical promotion of more inclusive ideals. These need to be offered as attractive and living alternatives that provide an equivalent sense of belonging but without the xenophobic component. In fostering academic and group cultures that actually embody the values they profess, it is essential to transcend the enumeration of "politically correct" attitudes and behaviours and to demonstrate fairness and conciliation in action.

A growing emphasis on individual and group "rights" has undoubtedly provoked some conflicts and encouraged more aggressive forms of group interaction and political dissent. It therefore becomes a major educational task to convince average citizens, young and old, that mechanisms exist to protect their interest in an impartial and expeditious manner and to resolve their conflicts without useless confrontations. In short, there are cracks not just in our systems to democratic and social participation but also in our systems of public protection and justice. To provide education in the rights and responsibilities of citizenship we must first define more clearly what these are but, no less importantly, we must show our citizens how they work and why they may be trusted to ensure the social peace.

Conclusion

Population and environmental pressures, pockets of political turmoil, huge economic disparities and the proliferation of devastating weaponry - these are among the more obvious threats to humane values in the twenty—first century. Such facts are themselves a major and irreducible part of the content of the life experience for which our "education", in the broadest sense, must prepare us. The main difficulty facing democratic and pluralistic cultures is that they have yet to prove that they can moderate, let along overcome, such threats without compromising or abandoning their declared principles. Educational approaches toward the goal of "responsible participation in a pluralistic society" must therefore reflect at least three things : (1) a comprehensive and credible programme for dealing with these global evils; (2) a substantially revised conception of the educational processes that will render them fully participatory and technically current; (3) much fuller development and refinement of the mechanisms for protecting the reconciling the equality and opportunity rights to which we are committed.

Mr Maxwell Yalden
Chief Commissioner
Canadian Human Rights Commission
320 Queen Street, 14th Floor, Place de Ville
Place de Ville, Tower A
Ottawa (Ontario) - Canada K1A 1E1

(Source: International Commission on Education for the Twenty First Century)

15

Adult Education and Lifelong Learning : Issues, Concerns and Recommendations of ICAE

— *A. M. Quiroz, J. L. Coraggio, H. Hinzen & R. M. Torres*

Education is undergoing a world-wide crisis. Adult education is part of that crisis, recognized as such by its own community. However, we see this crisis not as a breakdown, but rather as a challenge and as an opportunity for a strong new beginning. Adult education is vital for children's education, because it is adults — parents, teachers, politicians, technicians, ruling parties etc. — who are in charge of educating children at home, in school and through the media, and deciding what, how and why children need to learn. Hence, the usual dichotomy between children's education versus adult education (usually expressed in terms of allocation of resources, especially when these are scarce) is a false dichotomy.

The emphasis placed on girls, and women's education has not been accompanied by the necessary increase in financial resources. The support systems and measures necessary to ensure the participation of women are being ignored as well. Primary (children's) education seems to be winning the battle with basic education, to the detriment of adult education. Playing one age sector against another is not the right approach if the goal is to achieve education for all.

Lifelong learning is a prerequisite for today's society, and even more so for the future. It has implications for schools and institutions of higher learning as well as adult education institutions :

- Schools build on what children have learned in their families, in kindergarten, and in their peer groups, but most important is the school's contribution to children's motivation and ability to continue learning;
- Institutions of higher education should not be seen as the provider of the last cycle of education for the privileged few, but as a mass system for an ever-growing number of adults upgrading their knowledge and skills;
- Adult education, in all its different facets and approaches, already deals with the majority of the people in society, since we are all younger or older adults, or children who will become adults in due course.

There is currently much talk about **demand-driven education**, but the problem remains as to who will pose the demands, by which procedures, and what relation they will have with the subjective and objective needs of individuals, communities and society. The market has already proven to be a poor guide for investments, and cannot guide education and better. Private enterprise a well as consumers tend to think in terms of immediate needs which do not serve long-range goals well. There is a need for a strategic view which can only come from social reflection and prospect analysis that must be undertaken by State institutions. We must remember that in social science, more than in natural sciences, reflection and analysis must be accompanied by actions that help to make the ideas a reality. Thus, we need the resolve to shape the world and no merely contemplate the tragedy of billions. As has always been the case, a discussion centered on education is, in the end, also a discussion on what kind of society we dare to hope for.

When education is pursued as a sectoral policy *per se*, it can cause harm and have undesired effects. For instance **universal basic education** without a change in the strategies of production and accumulation of the corporate world and the State may produce a further depression in salaries and wages due to the excess supply of labour on a global scale. Instead of empowering the people, it could force them to complete for a reduced number of quality jobs.

Even though **basic education** is intended to lay the foundations of knowledge upon which all other learning through life would be built, it is a very difficult target to reach. The content of basic education constantly changes just as our world is constantly changing. In many cases the attention given by governments to basic education has resulted in educing the provision of education to its minimal level thereby degrading adult education.

Education appears as a possible penacea for the problems of the world. Among other things, the education system should deliver equity, productivity, citizenship, tolerance, and development. Although any meaningful breakthrough in those areas has an educational dimension, only an **integrated approach** would be efficient. This means other types of economic and social reforms, extending property rights and accepting other types of property apart from individual property, establishment of a more humane relationship between productivity and access to basic needs, democratization of political power, and development of appropriate technologies etc.

Lifelong learning, emphasized strongly in the last couple of years (and in the Faure report itself, 20 years ago) is far from becoming a reality or even being systematically included in policy development and programming. Lifelong learning is the framework within which adult education needs to be understood, but it is not limited to the adult world. It embraces childhood, youth and adulthood, and should embrace all learning environments and learning opportunities (i.e., home, work, school, media etc.). Thus there is a need to differentiate between lifelong **education** and lifelong **learning** (and adult **education** and adult **learning**). Learning occurs even in the absence of a systematic education process, outside schools and formal education settings. Therefore, it is essential to recognize, emphasize, and at the same time, differentiate the various learning environments and opportunities as well as the importance of revising conventional classifications such as those of formal, non-formal and informal education, which no longer belong to well-defined educational realities. Rather, they contribute to artificially separate what is actually an educational continuum.

Adult education must become a more **open and flexible system** that incorporates less conventional media such as self directed learning, distance education, and new technologies. The learning opportunities through the media must be acknowledged. By using these means, adult education can improve access and provision of programmes to those who have traditionally not taken part in it for any number of reasons. The code of conduct of our profession asks for a life long perspective in the training of trainers, teachers, and organizers involved in adult education. They have to update their knowledge, to improve and broaden their skills, and learn to cope with frustrations on the job long before burn-out occurs.

If adults are to learn to participate in development, decision-making at their places of work, or becoming self-reliant and responsible citizens, participatory methods and approaches are essential. If creativity in finding solutions to complex situations is increasingly required in the world of adult life, then this should determine the processes of lifelong learning and education. The Education for All Initiative, with its broader vision of basic education, understood as the education which meets the basic learning needs of children, youth and adults, provided a new conceptual and operational framework for adult education, recognizing adults' basic learning needs with the same legitimacy and urgency as those of children and youth. Jomtien's Declaration and framework for Action also stressed other important elements such as the need for intersectoral approaches to education (supportive policies to enhance learning environments and conditions) and new alliances and partnerships.

Adult education is not limited to adult literacy nor is it education for the poor. It should not be seen as a compensatory social policy to alleviate poverty, but rather as a tool for human development and self-reliance (human capital). Adult education must be all-inclusive by including people of all ages, genders, ethnic and social backgrounds. It must take into account the numerous aspects of lives and identities of the individuals (i.e. citizens, parents, care givers, workers, educators, consumers) and needs to incorporate the learning needs of all adults in all their capacities, Women, in particular, need to be seen not only as mothers or housewives but, first of all, as persons, Immigrants and refugees have identities beyond their labels as such and need to be not only respected, but appreciated in those capacities.

Although the number of illiterates in the total world population is decreasing, the rate of female illiteracy is still higher than male. Sufficient research has been accumulated to demonstrate the implications of female illiteracy for social change and economic development, for population growth and health and on the relationship between the mother's literacy and the education of the child. More efforts and resources should be concentrated on dealing with male/female literacy disparity. We also know that it is mainly women who are attending the literacy classes when available. There is not sufficient data as to what motivates them, whether they are able to maintain their attendance and interest, how appropriate are the materials used, etc.

The conventional notion of literacy/literate needs a thorough revision. Being able to read and write a simple statement of everyday life is not enough to prepare people to face the complexities of the modern world, much less those of the 21st century. Literacy itself is a lifelong learning process - **an ever moving target**. The abundant knowledge produced in recent years in the field of children's literacy has hardly been disseminated and incorporated into the field of adult education. The recent contribution of linguists, psychologists, and ethnographers has not been sufficiently considered.

The **integration of all adult education**, including general, political, cultural, and vocational education into a lifelong perspective is essential. We must overcome false assumptions and dichotomies: ■ technical training and re-training go together with the acquisition of social skills; ■key vocational qualifications include learning, communication, and analytical skills on and for all levels; ■ learning needs of the individual are increasingly the learning need of the society; ■ there is no ultimate knowledge and know-how; ■ personal growth should interact with and strengthen social developments; ■ the improvement of quality should not weaken the commitment and provision of education for all and; ■ national efforts should not undermine local, community oriented structures and their requirements.

In adult education, as in other fields, we need to look at **new partnerships** as well as old responsibilities. Public institutions and private companies, voluntary organizations and professional associations, and initiatives in related fields have to share their experiences, and they can all give new life to adult continuing education, including research of the universities and research institutes. Competition and market forces must not prevent co-operation. Moreover, governments must provide constructive legislation and a framework and logistical support which is conducive to the momentous tasks of the next decades which will see more adults living in this world than ever before.

Further Reading

Duke, Chris (ed.). *International Journal of University Adult Education,* IJUAE, New Brunswick.

Hinzen, Heribert (ed.). *Adult Education and Development.* 11Z/DVV, Bonn.

Jarvies, Peter (ed.). *International Journal of Lifelong Education.* Taylor & Francis, London.

Yarmol Franko, Karen (ed.) *Convergence,* ICAE, Toronto.

Ana María Quiroz, José Luis Coraggio, Heribert Hinzen and Rosa María Torres
International Council for Adult Education (ICAE)
720 Bathurst St. Suite 500
Toronto, Ontario
Canada M5S2R4

16

Policies and Legislation in Favour of Adult Education

— *P. Federighi*

The past decade has seen a marked increase in public and private intervention in the field of adult education by central, regional and local government departments and by private bodies of all kinds. Adult education has become a strategic factor in the management of human resources for economic and social development. But in whatever guise, at least in the most developed areas, adult education has become an arena for action.

Our research for UNESCO on state legislation in many countries throughout the world and on the real circumstances in which adult education bodies are working in Europe has enabled us to single out some fundamental trends.

The Transnational Dimension: The emergence and developing structure of a transnational dimension to education, directly linked to individual and local training arrangements is one of the most important trends.

A common European educational environment has gradually taken shape, undoubtedly in the wake of the informal educational influence of forces such as the market, the free movement of labour, migrations, of the educational potential of telecommunications. But today this dimension is apparent in the responsibilities and procedures brought into play, the plurality of decision-making centres, the funds invested, the facilities used, the sector of the public involved, the personnel employed and the infrastructure available. Despite limited resources, and, above all, in compliance with the so-called principle of 'subsidiarity' - whereby action for which national policies do not provide must be ruled out - we are now witnessing the construction of an autonomous transnational system of adult education.

In this context, approaches have been developed which are not new as far as adult education is concerned, but which are certainly innovative in relation to institutional strategies. It is against this background that we should analyze and reformulate, rather than taking on trust, the new meaning permeating relations between Eastern and Western Europe and between Europe and the Third World. In this sphere, too, we are witnessing an unprecedented strengthening of bonds. Programmes, treaties and conventions - bilateral and multilateral- have become legion. These trends have been shaped by two opposing influences: on the one hand, an educational explosion, and on the other, expansion of aid programmes.

Adult Education and the World of Production : Here, the leading tendency seems to be to encourage the development of processes already under way in the programmes of the world of adult education: (a) to set up **local systems** of adult education with the aim of overcoming the fragmentation of the types of training on offer and the stratification of possibilities of access to such training; (b) to promote activities specifically geared to the **development of entrepreneurial and vocational abilities**, with particular reference to the world of small and medium-sized businesses and in rural areas; (c) to develop activities of **basic scientific training,** and indeed all activities designed to raise general educational standards, from elementary to university levels; (d) to **anticipate** how much adult education still has to accomplish in order to mitigate the revolution in methods of production.

National, Regional and Local Policies and the Rise of Associations: The question of the legislation needed to guarantee direct access to education is on the agenda of all democratic countries. National and regional governments must be supported in the task of working out a new normative framework for the right to adult education. A combined effort of information exchange, research and testing of the effectiveness of various types of legislative and administrative measures seems to us to be an objective for the immediate future, both for public institutions and for the adult education movement.

Of equal urgency is support at the local level for the planning and management of interventions, which will play an increasingly large part in all countries. It is at the local level that the dynamics of educational demand can best be monitored and effective forms of social management introduced.

The Adult Education System: Supporting the development of national adult education systems that are functional and effective means intervening in the renovation of their individual components. The following are just some of the areas most concerned by such renewal: (a) development of action in the field of secondary education; (b) reconversion of residential centres; (c) introduction of new technologies and new forms of distance education (d) improvement of cultural infrastructures to cater for the educational needs of the adult population (museums, libraries, etc.; (e) training needs, at present only partly satisfied, of participants working at transnational, university or association level; (f) development of basic services (guidance, information, etc.); (g) introduction of forms of certification attesting to knowledge acquired.

Access to Adult Education : The issue of access to education, or of the distribution of educational or cultural goods, is one that we mention in conclusion only to emphasize how far it affected all these areas of work. After years of compartmentalized educational supply there seem to be trends pointing in another direction. The trend is to encourage specialization but without the creation of subsystems favouring segregation of learners and their inevitable marginalization (the elderly, immigrants, the young, etc.) The problem to be tackled is that of opening up the existing adult education system to meet the educational needs of the full range of learners in the population.

Further Reading

Federighi, P. (1990). Administrative and Legislative Measures in Favour of Adult Education. Florence, University of Florence.

European Bureau of Adult Education (1993). Adult Education Organizations in Europe. Barcelona, EBEA-EAEA.

P. Federighi

for

International Council on Adult Education (ICAE)

720 Bathurst St., Suite 500

Toronto, Ontario Canada M5S 2R4

(Source: International Commission on Education for the Twenty First Century)

17

Peace Education in Adult Education

— Helena Kekkonen

Many wars all over the world are proof of the observation that pro-war and pro-violence attitudes continue to prevail. International research has revealed that the primary obstacles to achieving peace are the erroneous prejudices and biased attitudes that have become rooted in the minds of people. One of these is the conception that national and ethnic culture and identity are best defended by taking up arms. The willingness to develop alternative, non-violent defense methods has been lacking.

There has been conscious neglect in political quarters of the fact that rearmament uses up the world's natural resources, that the use of this equipment pollutes the environment, and that rearmament uses up resources that might otherwise be used to solve problems. The poverty, hunger and debt afflicting developing countries and social inequality are the greatest threats in tomorrow's world. Peace education is needed more than ever for children youth and adults.

Peace education is based on our adapting a global way of thinking and of giving consideration to ethical principles. It consists of three phases: *knowledge*, changing of attitudes and practical peace actions. *Knowledge* is needed on understanding of the causes of wars in other that we might learn to repel them in time. In trying to achieve a state of peace the removal of so-called structural violence (like hunger, undernourishment, inequalities between nations) and violations of human rights is necessary. Reduction of armaments could give resources and solve global problems just mentioned. Knowledge is also needed on the past application of non-violent opposition with fresh, modern approaches being developed at the same time. People are taught negotiation skills needed in clearing up conflict situations.

Peace educations deals with the manifestations of psychological warfare preceding actual wars. The student is taught how to recognize these and how to oppose them. Examples of creations of the pictures of the enemy are examined and attempts are made to enter "the opposite culture": i.e. to understand the way of thinking, customs and history of foreign peoples in order that understanding the basic similarity between peoples might do away with the concept of "enemy". Peace education means learning to trust in the common sense that people have and non-acceptance of old, fixed beliefs such as "security", "defence" and "heroism".

Research work in the field of education has proved that even the best of knowledge does not always have the desired effect. Knowledge on its own does not ensure changes in attitudes and behaviour. Peace education aims at knowledge being "internalized", at the "conscientization" of knowledge, the term used by Paolo Freire. Are IQs essential for this to be achieved. Peace education aims at retaining children's and young people's capacity for empathy (genuine sympathy) in place of emphatic rationality and one-sided development of what is thought to be sensibility. Thus, the versatile employment of art is part of cooperation and peace pedagogics that emphasizes personal responsibility. Fiction, poems, films, theatre and music open up new vistas into strange cultures. In so doing, they influence our feelings - enabling us to identify with people suffering because of war, hunger or poverty.

Experience has shown that knowledge and art together as the core of peace education have inspired people to take action. The participants decide for themselves how they can best work for the goal of lasting peace. Some people are engaged in development cooperation, some in human rights matters, others strive to save the environment or to do away with other injustices. Improving the lot of women and children in the developing countries is a central theme in peace education.

The target groups in peace education (e.g. in the case of Finland and other Nordic countries) are as follows :

1. Teachers in comprehensive schools and secondary schools : The aim has been to give these people adequate grounding in implementing peace education among children and young people and thereby reach entire age classes.

In actual fact, the only condition for the implementation of peace education is to make the educators personally aware of the necessity of peace education. Peace education is not the same for everyone nor is it tied to any general sets of instructions. It must be adapted to each educator's own personality; it is creative work. In many countries there is an abundance of literature on peace education for the purpose of widening one's knowledge base and for providing practical stimuli to learning situations. The developing countries do need support in this respect.

An especially important target group is trainee teachers.

2. Parents of pupils : Successful peace education requires cooperation with the children's parents.

3. Pupils at comprehensive schools and secondary schools. Theme days and theme weeks are organized and support is given to action days which focus on specific development cooperation targets. Mostly the other party in the cooperation situation is a school from a developing

country or a non-governmental organization acting on an environmental issue (e.g. to prevent desertification.)

4. Adult educators at all levels : Adult educators pass on knowledge on peace education to all kinds of non-governmental organizations.

5. Representatives of the media : Peace educations on television, radio and in the press has generated public debate and thereby helped to promote the gradual achieving of peace education's goals.

The ongoing wars are proof of the fact that peace education has not yet achieved the set goals, but also of the gradual changes in attitudes. There are also some positive results indicating a gradual increase in people's awareness.

The objective of peace education in adult education is to awaken the ethical consciousness and the profound consideration of human values, to make a person sensitive to injustice and misery and to activate for concrete measures.

Peace education in practice means that each individual is encouraged to develop into a critically thinking citizen (one that does not blindly obey the authorities and one that does not comply with everything just to be "tolerant"), bold in action, capable of cooperation with others, and one whose life values are based on respecting the life of every human being and on striving to ensure that the nature about us is passed on to future generations.

Further Reading

No limits to learning, 1979. Botkin, J.W. et al., Pergamon Oxford.

The first global revolution, 1991. King, A., Schneider, B., Simon & Schuster London.

A window onto the future, 1986. Kekkonen, H., AFAEO,

Uusikaupunki, Finland.

Recommendation on the development of adult education, 1976. UNESCO, Nairobi.

Peace, environment and education, 2/1991 and 4/1993, IPRA, Malmo, Sweden.

Directions in the study of peace education, 1991. ed. Calleja, J. et al. SAID, Valletta, Malta.

Helena Kekkonen
Vice-Chairman of Peace Education Institute
Vattuniemenk, 18 F 115
00210 Helsinki
Finland

(Source: International Commission on Education for the Twenty First Century)

18

Education and Literacy: The Case for Partnership Building and Networking

— Lalita Ramdas

Introduction

For the past several decades, the problems of universalisation of elementary education and achievement of a totally literate society in large parts of the developing world have continued to concern governments, citizens and non-governmental organisations alike. The answers are still elusive. In the recent past the Jomtien Conference on Education for All and the Largest Country Initiative represent two major global initiatives in Education. The challenge today, clearly is how to translate both global and national policy objectives into concrete action on the ground.

Experience has shown that neither governments nor NGOs alone have been able to deliver the goods with regard to Education and Development.

The high expectations from partnership building have floundered. Vast resources and huge formal schooling systems have not necessarily yielded results.

Perhaps future policy and practice needs to take into consideration some of the following : (a) highly centralized models of education no longer work especially in many non-industrialized societies; (b) decentralized, micro-systems and innovations need to be encouraged, understood, reorganized and networked into a loose knot federation for education for all; (c) local self-government bodies need to be catalyzed and given the necessary information, skills and inspiration to build, plan and run educational programmes and institutions in local areas; (d) women, especially mothers, should be both motivated and trained much more than they are at present, to take an active role in moulding their vision for educating themselves and their children; (e) resources need to be placed in the hands of responsible people at the local levels. Local resources need to be identified and mobilized; (f) larger scale, donor-to-government funding for inputs into education, needs much more careful scrutiny. Lack of material and financial resources are not the primary source of the problem they represent but only one aspect. Pouring resources into sectors which will be managed by existing, inefficient or corrupt infra-structure can *never* deliver the goods; (g) existing resources, especially by way of teachers' associations, need special attention, motivation and re-orientation. It is here that a mass campaign, a mass awareness and education movement needs to be designed and put in place; (h) bureaucrat and politician alike need to be educated to these new realities; (i) new inter sectoral and inter-disciplinary coalitions must emerge to play major advocacy roles within nation states; (j) the existing surplus of human, infrastructural and even material resources in private, corporate, business and government and defense services needs to be harnessed and brought into a national pool of resources with a single point focus on education over the next decade; (k) political leaders need to lead and articulate a vision for a self-reliant, educated and skilled human resource base; (l) current economic policies, dictated by a highly inward-looking and conservative coalition of mega institutions located in the industrialized North, need serious and drastic re-examination. This alone can enable the integration of the principle of economic self-reliance and educational goals into a common workable vision.

Conclusion

The agenda for the twenty-first century should be one of review and reflection. A policy of providing time and resources to building true democracy and a highly developed human resource base from the grass roots up is in the long run the only answer to effective and relevant education in practice.

Further Reading

UNESCO, 1993. Report on Education for All, Status & Trends, Paris

WCEFA, 1990-92 Final Reports and Documents. Jomtien

UNICEF, 1993. Report on EFA Consultation. New York.

UNICEF, 1993. Reaching the Unreached (UNICEF Paper). New York

UNDP, 1991, Human Development Report, New York

UNICEF, 1992. State of the World's Children

UNICEF, 1991. Situation Analysis of Women and Children in India. New York

ICAE, 1991. ICAE Journal Convergence, Vol. XXIV, no. 4. Toronto

Ramdas, Lalita, 1992. Women's Literacy : Equity & Relevance (paper presented to UNESCO Conference on Urban Literacy)

Ramdas, Lalita, 1992. Mobilising Partnerships for Education for All-UNESCO Seminar, Colombo.

Ramdas, Lalita, 1991. The Challenge of Poverty and the Role of Education.

Lalita Ramdas, New Delhi, India
for International Council on Adult Education (ICAE)
720 Bathrust St., Suite 500
Toronto, Ontario - Canada M5S 2R4

(Source: International Commission on Education for the Twenty First Century)

19

Renewing Physical Education for the Future

— *J. E. Kane*

Introduction

There is growing demand across the world for increased and relevant educational opportunity. In satisfying this demand, education will necessarily need to reflect the requirement of the fast advancing microtechnological revolution and the highly competitive economic marketplace. More generally, however, the changing face of education for the twenty-first century will need to accommodate the individual's needs to communicate satisfactorily, to process information, to solve problems, to harmonize with the environment and, above all, to be set firmly on the road of opportunity to becoming personally fulfilled. It is about the process and the product of personal fulfilment that physical education (and sports education) will be increasingly concerned with as we enter the next millennium. This objective will involve equipping the individual to become all that he/she is capable of becoming in the context of an agreeable human existence. The vital contribution of the physical education curriculum begins with the development of clear ideas of the "instrumental body" and proceeds to shaping positive and purposeful body concepts and self-concepts. From such solid foundations it is hoped that feelings and behaviours associated with self concepts. From such solid foundations it is hoped that feeling and behaviours associated with self-competence, self-assurance and self-fulfilment will be effectively shaped in a 'new' education charter for 'new' people.

Health-Related Fitness

Increasingly, programmes of physical education have taken on responsibility for teaching school children about health and fitness. Such purposes may be regarded by the philosophers as extrinsic or instrumental to the main purposes of education. Nevertheless, one can understand why physical education teachers have adopted this important area of preparation for life where the focus is in the continuing concern for the care and functioning capacity of the body systems. Teachers need to relate the provision of education for health related fitness in the school curriculum to subsequent practice and above all not to regard this provision as a substitute for an integrated programme of physical education which has, or ought to have, wider and more intrinsic purposes. With those pints made, it may well be that teachers of physical education should and will develop an appropriate rationale and capacity for establishing the foundation for self-care of the functioning body since body image and body concepts are likely in the future to play an even greater part in the psychology of personal stability which underpins personality and social effectiveness.

Sport and physical education have long laid claim to moral education widely interpreted (McIntosh). Such moral virtues as honesty, co-operativeness, friendship and fair play are fundamental to the true notion of sport and *homo ludens* and are enshrined in the charter purposes of the Olympic movement. The ICSSPE links with the International Olympic Committee in promoting these virtues together with others aimed at advancing peace and international understanding. Moreover, the ICSSPE sustains an International Fair Play Committee whose purpose is to identify and command exemplary behaviour in sporting contests focused on foul play.

It would seem that sport and physical education is uniquely placed to inculcate best practice in many of the moral virtues and others which are related and desirable, but clearly efforts and resources will need to be increased significantly to have a greater impact. Moreover, a great deal of further research will be required here to identify the best pedagogic methods to achieve greater success.

Aesthetics and Creativity

From the broad definition given above of education as being focused on pursuits which are intrinsically satisfying and valuable we can anticipate a greater contribution in the future from creative body movement as in dance. Such opportunities can add important dimensions to (high) cultural development and to both satisfaction and fulfilments through creative body mastery. Experience of this kind of body control and management represents (though not exclusively) what Pring proposed as 'practical knowledge—a concept that has much to offer the imaginative curriculum planners of the twenty-first century. The body-in-movement mode of aesthetic experience is linked with but different from other forms of creativity like painting or music-making and will be increasingly valued as making a unique contribution to the rounded education of 'new' people.

Quality of Life

The term "quality of life" has quite different connotations for those living in the North and South of the world. For both however education represents the means of achieving a better quality of life. In the south (and particularly in the large tracts of Africa) many live at the margins of life through lack of adequate resources but even in these impoverished areas the constant and fundamental plea is for improved educational systems and especially literacy. For those who cannot read there is the multiple impoverishement resulting from the insecurity of diminished communication and their exclusion from the comforts and delights of the written word. Only after massive resources have been allocated and good management systems established can we hope to secure even basic education for all; within which we should dedicate our expertise in sports and physical education. The young people in particular may be attracted to the joy and pleasure in games, sports and dance from which self-identity via competence may be forged and self-assurance and ambition developed. The ICSSP has committed its organization to promote these quality of life objectives in the twenty first century.

In the north of the world and especially in the developed industrialized countries education *is* quality of life which is widely interpreted as the agreeability of urban man's environment - and especially the suitability of the environment for the realization of the individual's human potential. Education, in this connection, opens up new horizons for the fuller use of potential leading to achievement and satisfactions of a higher and higher order. In this process education is being increasingly described in terms of providing the progressive opportunities for self-actualization (Maslow). The emphasis here is on personal satisfaction, meaning fulfilment, levels of conscientiousness and joy which (for the psychologist) are the elements subscribing to the intrinsically motivated person in the pursuit of 'feeling competent' and 'self determining' in relation to his environment. These are the issues which are becoming the centre of the debate and the focus of planning for curriculum programmes in sport and physical education. As we generate more momentum in shaping our plans for the twenty-first century, we can be assured that these notions emphasizing the sensitive progress of human development towards self-actualization and life quality will be increasing importance.

There is a growing sense among scholars that the place of physical education in the curriculum is ripe for reappraisal. The basis for a relevant curriculum will emphasize the basis for the development through the "instrumental body" of concepts of self-competence and self-fulfilment. In shaping the curriculum for the twenty-first century educationists will be wise to recognize the importance of the post-modern youth culture. Governments should consider the very special contribution that can be made by physical education in the context of a rounded education for life.

Further Reading

King, E. 1977. *Re-organising Education*, Sage Publs., London

Maslow, A.H. 1970, *Motivation & Personality*. Harper, New York.

McIntosh, P. 1979, *Fair Play : Ethics in Sport and Education*. Heinemann. London

Tinning, R. and Fitzclarence, L. 1992. Postmodern Youth Culture and the Crisis in Australian Secondary School Physical Education, *Quest*, Vol. 44, No. 3 P. 287-303. Dec. 1992. Human Kinetics Publishers for National Associations. Association for PE in HE (NAPEHE)

Tedesco, J.C. 1993 *Current trends in Education Reform*. UNESCO Meeting Document, EDC. 93/CNF. 001.1.4

J.E. Kane
International Council of Sports Science and Physical Education (ICSSPE)
University of Jyväskylä
PL 35-SF-40351 Jyväskýlä, Finland

(Source: International Commission on Education for the Twenty First Century)

20

Prisoner Education

— *Stephen Duguid*

Introduction

The provision of education for adults in prisons is a task in constant need of justification. Unlike most clients of adult or higher education, prisoners are either: (a) perceived to be deserving of punishment and thus further deprivation of basic services and rights and, coincidentally, unlikely to profit from learning opportunities, (b) due to social backgrounds or psychological deprivation best suited for education and vocational training or (c) in need of specialized "treatment" or interventions designed to reduce their propensity to re-offend. Educators in prisons, therefore must constantly argue for the vocation and in the process of doing so have reached divergent though sometimes complementary positions. For instance, in responses to the "nothing works" view of prisoners and prisons, many educators focus on the ameliorative effect of education on the management of the prison. Others have made a strong case for "schooling" in the prison as response to the educational and cultural deprivation found amongst the imprisoned while the more economistic make a strong case for vocational training. The more optimistic assert the primacy or at least participation of education in the rehabilitative/reformative agenda of the prison.

Prison education may suffer from being an oxymoron. Prisons are authoritatrian institutions and except for the more pathological amongst us, seen as universally undesirable, albeit necessary, institutions. They rely on coercion, manipulation and brute force to contain humans for specified periods of time and in many cases include in their ethos if not their mandate the provision of punishment beyond the fact of incarceration itself. They are traditionally underfunded by governments and ignored by the public except as sources of employment and deterrence. Education, on the other hand, is generally seen as liberating, dependent on the free flow of ideas and, in the case of adults, dependent on opportunities to put into practice ideas and skills learned in the classroom.

Despite these apparent contradictions there has grown up over the past century or more a subset of adult education called "prison education" (or, in the United States, "correctional education"). The practice of education in prison varies considerably depending on factors such as the resources available, the ideology of the political/correctional system, and the health of the various correctional intervention programmes at any given time. Thus, like education in general, though perhaps more overtly, education in prisons is always a "second order" activity and tends to be reactive rather than proactive. In those nations seen to be "developing" the provision of education in prisons is a low national priority. Educational resources are scarce, teachers poorly trained and prisons too often in abysmal conditions. Due to these situations "schooling" is the dominant form of education, particularly literacy and basic life skills. Necessity sometimes being the "parent" of invention, many exciting and innovative literacy and basic education initiatives have emerged from these settings, particularly those which involve the local community in the prison education enterprise.

Conclusion

In the nations of the former and existing "socialist world" prison education has been a formal partner in the reformative mandate given to prisons. "Re-education", a concept that sits uncomfortably in a post-Orwellian world, is the order of the day in prison systems based on the premise that crime must be a deviation caused by ignorance rather than by social or cultural deprivation. Education in prisons is an important tool in the effort to have prisoners come to see the "error of their ways".

In the "developed" nations of the West the practice varies depending on the operative paradigm, which is itself driven by politics, finances and research. In past years the dominant role for education has been "schooling", specifically the delivery of literacy, secondary school and vocational education programmes. The rationale for such programmes rested on a complex series of explanations for crime, resting mostly on sociological foundations. More recently the rationale has begun to shift back to psychological causes for crime and hence education programmes are being asked to serve more specific ends such as addressing addiction, violence, anger and sexual deviation.

In the past decade prison educators around the world have emerged from their isolated and isolating institutions and discovered a common vocation amidst divergent theories and praxis. A series of international meetings in the United States, Canada, England, Sweden, Estonia and Holland has created a discourse community of teachers, administrators and researchers. Such a community is an essential first step in creating a profession that can withstand the vagaries of political and ideological shifts in states 'thinking about crime and punishment and, while cognizant of cultural diversity, strive toward some common standards for education in prison.

Further Reading

Yearbook of Correctional Education, 1989, 1990, 1991, 1992. Available from the Institute for the Humanities, Simon Fraser University, Burnaby, British Colombia, Canada V5A 1S6

Education in Prison, 1990. Recommendation number R(89)12. Adopted by the Council of Europe, 1989 and explanatory memorandum.

Stephen Duguid
Simon Fraser University
Burnaby, B.C.
Canada V5A 1S6

(Source: International Commission on Education for the Twenty First Century)

21

An Institute of Environmental Sciences : A Proactive Effort for Community Improvement

—*J. Roy-Poirier*

In 1991, a Canadian community of Eastern Ontario launched an ambitious project through the intermediary of its satellite University of Ottawa campus to broaden the horizons of university education within its milieu. The main objective of the plan is to develop a unique and different research and study programme within an institute of environmental sciences. Nestled on the broad banks of the St. Lawrence River, the Institute is intended to become a world-class facility dedicated to the study of large river aquatic ecosystems and environmental conditions. The publicly-owned institute is being developed by four partners: a medium-sized Canadian city with a population of 47,000, the neighbouring Mohawk community of Akwesasne, the three adjoining counties and a major Canadian University, the University of Ottawa. Escalating concern for the environment has been one motivating factor in the choice of this particular project. Also, from a community point of view, a socio-economic crisis brought about by a prolonged Canadian recession has led the local leaders to look carefully at positive solutions to a difficult situation. The involved city has an unemployment rate of 22%, a 40% dependency on social assistance, a growing rate of criminal activity and violence with an accompanying family-related degree of poverty and personal trauma. Unemployment has been brought about mainly by the closure of several manufactures within this principally blue-collar city and its surrounding community. Solutions to these work-related problems are being sought through educational means, combining education and work.

Although the project has progressed at a somewhat moderate pace, accomplishments to date include: the acquisition by the University of Ottawa of a $2.25 million grant under the Canadian Green Plan fund for the recovery of the St. Lawrence River system, the creation of a Board of Directors for the Institute. Incorporation is also in the process as well as the hiring of personnel to include an Empowerment Project director, a management trainee and secretarial staff. The planning of major fund-raising campaign is also in the process. A detailed business plan is about to be commissioned.

This institute means that an economically-depressed area of Canada will hopefully have more control over its own future, will better be able to care for its ecosystem, will have opportunities to develop and foster new technologies and industries. Most of all, it aims to expand its educational capacities and enhance the qualify of life of its citizens.

This experience and experiment is an attempt of an economically depressed Canadian bilingual (English and French) community to bring about major change within its milieu. It is a collaborative effort combining the efforts of a city of Eastern Ontario, the three surrounding counties and a university. A partnership has also been established with the adjoining Native Reserve of Akwesasne.

Further Reading

Botki, James W., et al. *On ne finit pas d'apprendre : le fossé humain á combler.* Pergamon Press. 1980.

Carrefour. Actes du colloque, Ethique et éducation á

distance. Ottawa Université d'Ottawa. 1988.

Dumont, René. *Un monde intolérable.* Paris, Editions du Seuil. 1988.

Enhancement and Diversification : An Economic Development Strategy for Cornwall in the 1990's, Final Report, submitted by Prospectus Investment and Trade Partners, Inc., 29 January 1990.

Knowles, Malcolm. *The Modern Practice of Adult Education : from pedagogy to andragogy.* New York, Cambridge, 1980.

Ms Jeannine Roy-Poirier
Canadian Association for the Study of Adult Education Organization
R.R. 3
Ingleside (ON) Canada KOC 1MO

(Source : International Commission on Education for the Twenty First Century)

22

Science and Mathematics Education in a New Social and Economic Context

— Graham Orpwood

Introduction

Science and mathematics have always been important areas of study both for students in elementary and secondary schools and for those in post-secondary institutions. However, as the 21st century draws closer, Canadians along with other citizens of the world, have a greater need than ever before of high quality science and mathematics. The rapidly changing context of education - including the economic, social, technological and political dimensions - require that much more attention be paid to science and mathematics than has traditionally been the case. These changing contexts dictate new goals, new content, new methods of teaching, and new ways of assessing progress in school and university science and mathematics. Overall, a new approach to learning is required.

Increasing global economic competition requires that countries (such as Canada) that depend on trade for their prosperity and standard of living, look more and more to high quality education in science and technology to spur industrial innovation. Thus, high achievement in math and science and the development of the skills and attitudes associated with creativity and innovation are critical. Yet, the curricula in science and mathematics and the methods of teaching used in schools are changing very slowly. In 1984 the Science Council of Canada presented a report entitled "Science for Every Student: Educating Canadians for Tomorrow's World." Since that time, some progress has been made but international comparisons remind us that much more is needed. Measuring progress in math and science is becoming an increasing priority in Canada.

Technology continues to dominate our work and personal lives, yet few in school learn to become technologically literate and the numbers of those entering engineering are at a plateau. The Science Council's 1984 Report opened with an endorsement of a statement in the 1972 Faure Commission Report, *Learning to Be* :

> *An understanding of technology is vital in the modern world and must be a part of everyone's basic education.*

The Council went on to comment : "there was international consensus on this point 12 years ago; yet little has happened, at least in North America". This is still true today. As the skills required for tomorrow's industry become more complex, preparing young people for the jobs of the future becomes more challenging. Cooperative education, in which this task is shared between schools and industry is becoming a poplar option in Canadian school systems as are other forms of partnership between schools and industry.

Socially, Canada has changed rapidly in the past twenty years and is facing the challenges of a multicultural society. Yet participation in science, technology and mathematics fails to reflect these changes. A growing, though still too small a number of women and members of visible minority groups including aboriginal people enter the science and engineering professions, thus creating a distorted and inequitable balance in our society. Teaching and assessment methods must change to take into account the rich variety of life experiences and conceptual backgrounds of all Canadians in full participation in these fields is to be achieved.

Progress is being made, however. Provincial education systems are beginning to conduct systematic assessments of students' progress in math and science.

Demands for grater political participation and the growing democratization of our social institutions has increased the need for all citizens to be literate in math, science, and technology. This has yet to be matched by appropriate senior levels of courses taken by all students through their high school years. New ways of understanding science and mathematics, set in real world contexts, must become standard for all students throughout their education and methods of assessment must reflect this need. Otherwise, as the Science Council pointed out, "if we, as a society, fail to understand the interaction of science, technology and society, we surrender control of the most potent forces shaping our world to a technocratic elite."

Science and mathematics are important because they make up an important dimension of 20th century life and culture, and a person who claims to be "liberally" or "humanistically" educated, must also be literate in math and science. This dimension of science education must not be forgotten in our need to remain competitive economically.

Conclusion

In the past decade, Canadians have become increasingly concerned with their system of public schooling. Canadian results in international tests have been discouraging. School systems have only reluctantly accepted the need for increased accountability and the pace of curricular and pedagogical innovation has been painfully slow. A recent national report has called for a "strong learning culture" that focuses on results, makes learning continuous, innovates to strengthen the systems and involves all Canadians (*Inventing Our Future*). Another has stressed the need for a more comprehensive system that integrates school, work and training more closely (*A Lot to Learn*). Yet our educational institutions are designed to meet the goals of the past. As a recent analysis of Canadian schools puts it.: "Canadian education is under stress... its external environment is changing faster than its internal workings can adapt" (*Overdue Assignment*).

Clearly, major structural and institutional changes are on the horizon for Canada's schools as they prepare for the 21st century. Mathematics and science are cornerstones of the society we live in today and an education system created in the 19th century will no longer do. Education in mathematics, science and technology for the 21st century must aim at both excellence and equity. It must fully integrate with the "real world" in which we live, and it must be lifelong in its scope.

Further Reading

A Lot to Learn : Education and Training in Canada, statement by the Economic Council of Canada, Ottawa, 1992.

Inventing Our Future : An Action Plan for Canada's Prosperity, Steering Group on Prosperity, Ottawa, 1992.

Learning Mathematics and Learning Science, International Assessment of Education Progress, Princeton, NJ, 1992.

Overdue Assignment : Taking Responsibility for Canada's Schools, by Jennifer Lewington and Graham Orpwood, John Wiley & Sons, Toronto, 1993.

School Achievement Indicators Program, Report on Mathematics Assessment, Council of Ministers of Education, Canada, Toronto 1993.

Science for Every Student : Educating Canadians for

Tomorrow's World, Report 36 of the Science Council of Canada, Ottawa 1984.

Dr. Graham Orpwood
Assistant Professor and Science Liaison Officer
Faculty of Education
York University
North York (Ontario)
Canada M3J IP3

(Source: International Commission on Education for the Twenty First Century)

23

Partnerships to Strengthen Science and Mathematics Education

— *Veronica Lacey*

Introduction

There exists currently an imperative for every citizen to have an education in science, mathematics and technology which is appropriate, is of the highest quality and focuses on an understanding of the connections of science, technology and society. What form does this best possible education take? How can it be afforded? How might the most appropriate teacher group be constituted, prepared and supported? In its submission to the Ontario Royal Commission on Learning, the North York Board of Education called for "the development of a comprehesive lifelong "learning culture" in Canada, based on partnerships in all sectors and all segments of society". The benefits to be derived from educational partnering for the learners, the schools and the partners themselves have been documented extensively. How might partnerships focused on science and technology help to address such questions as those above?

Several realities reinforce the urgency of developing a clear image of sciece and mathematics education. Equity of opportunity must be a simple principle of good practice - the "every citizen" above must mean exatly that. Debate continues both on the desirability and on the best ways of delivering both a scientific awareness for most and a thoroguh scientific preparation for a few. The rapid expansion in new knowledge is centred on science and technology while the explosion in new communications technology will change the ways we both generate knowledge and seek to understand it. The environment crises threatening our existence are generally seen to have both their genesis and their solutions rooted in science. The concept of career-long learning reflects a need a maintain understading of a complex existence continually re-created through technology.

Partnering in education resists easy definition. Students have long benefitted from having volunteers in the classroom and from the annual trip to the local fire station. Science fairs, public speaking competitions and essay-writing contests frequently present prizes donated by service clubs and other community groups. Cooperative education programs have provided opportunities for students to experience the workplace. Transitional programs have created new links among various educational institutions. More recently, however, the business sector in Canada has also begun to play a varied and creative role in education. The best possible science, mathematics and technology education will rely upon the broadest definition of partner business and labour organizations, community groups, post-secondary institutions and more. Further, partnerships will range from a single company linked with an individual school to a consortium of organizations connected with schools and school boards across the country. A mandate for partnering in science at the local and national (and international) level would address the following needs :

a) development of a national focus and consensus about science and mathematics education,

b) provision of the broadest range of resources,

c) design of appropriate experiences for students.

d) professional preparation of teachers in science and mathematics,

e) promotion of the value of science and of science education for individual and for society, and

f) implementation of a continuous assessment of partnering initiatives.

Derek Hodson describes three aspects of science education: learning science, learning about science and doing science. Through *learning science*, a student develops a conceptual framework of facts and principles to be used in understanding new ideas. Through *learning about science*, a student comes to an understanding of the rules, the processes and skills and the values associated with science. It is here that one also learns how science connects to other disciplines. *Doing science* refers to actual scientific inquiry and problem-solving, higher order thinking skills and, eventually, the creation of new knowledge. Hodson's delineation can be an effective model for science partenrs to use to structure support for the appropriate science program for any particular group of learners. It allows these planners to develop clear connections between a specific initiative and that aspects of a science program to be addressed. As an example, a monitoring program developed by a partnership might be designed with an understanding that its main purpose was to contribute to *learning about science* rather than to be a way of *learning science*.

Science as a career and the formal educational preparation required are perceived as "hard work" by many students and not worth the effort when so many other career options appear possible. Science partners must find ways to demonstrate the professional satisfaction and personal growth possible in scientific careers as well as the value of a scientific awareness for every member of society. They must contribute to support networks for students who choose careers in science or mathematics. The Shad Valley summer program in technology and entrepreneurship, operated by the Canadian Centre for Creative Technology, is a fine example of corporate support for students choosing to excel in this area. Although teaching science requires a certain level of background, too frequently, elementary teachers in particular have themselves received little formar science education. Partners can assist through the sponsorship of professional programs for teachers in science and by providing human resources to the process of teaching and learning. The Upjohn company in the United States offers a two-weed residential program, *Science Grasp*, for elementary teachers selected from across North America. In British Columbia, the *Recreational Science at Loon Lake* program, offered through Science World in Vancouver, is a similar experience for teachers from across Canada and received support from Merck Frost Canada. In Quebec the *Societe pour la promotion de la science et de la technologie* operates a programme of scientific sponsorship between schools and industrial firms. The federal *Innovators in the Schools* program provides clasroom volunteers to assist teachers with science.

New understandings in science demand easy access to the most current thinking, resources and technology available. Using the expertise of a team of teachers from the North York Board of Education, Connaught Laboratories led the development of a new teaching resource, *Biotechnology for a healtheir world*, to be made available across Canada. The international Society of Automotive Engineers (SAE) has developed a resource package, *Wheels in Motion*, designed for use in senior elementary classes with the participation of volunteer member of SAE.

The national network for learning is a unique partnership of school boards, post-secondary institutions and business corporations from across Canada. The NNL is closely connected with many other related educational network projects such as School Net to share emerging understandings of teaching and learning about science and mathematics through the use of technology. Teachers and students using the network will collaborate in research and development to create curriculum of high educational value. Canadians are naturally proud of our leadership in the area of communications technology. The future will reveal educational partnerships in this field providing yet to be imagined opportunities for students.

Conclusion

Educational partnering raises questions of jurisdiction and appropriateness. In the focus truly on the achievement of students ? Is a particular learning resource offered by a partner acceptable in the schools' context? Is it clear that accountability and responsibility for program rest with the school? These questions represent challenges. They need not be barriers. Partnerships in scinece can move beyond the bounds of schools and the restrictions of static resources. Partnerships in science can address the essential connnection among the accumulated knowledge of science, the impact of technology and the issues confronting society. Partnerships in science can help take students and their teachers to the edges of understanding as learners and as contributors.

Further Reading

Hirsch, Donald. (1992) Centre for Educational Research and Innovation. *Schools and Business : a new partnership*, Paris.

Hodson, D. (1993). Taking A Critical Look at Laboratory Work. *Crucible, Magazine of the Science Teachers' Association of Ontario* 6, 12-15.

North York Board of Education. (1993) *Submission to the Ontario Royal Commission on Learning.* North York.

Steering Group on Prospeirty. (1992) *Inventing Our Future: An Action Plan for Canada's Prosperity.* Ottawa.

The Canadian Chamber of Commerce. (1990) *Focus 2000 Business Education Partnerships.*

Your Planning Process Guide. Ottawa.

National Network for Learning. Further information is

available by contacting the North York Board of Education, 5050 Yonge Street, North York, On M2N 5N8 Tel : (416) 395 8481.

Ms Veronica Lacey
Director, Education
North York Board of Education
5050 Yonge Street
North York (Ontario)
Canada M2N 5N8

(Source: International Commission on Education on the Twenty First Century)

24

Measuring Success in Science and Mathematics Education

— Denis Savard

Introduction

The teaching of science and mathematics will necessarily undergo substantial changes during the next few years. The object of these changes is to develop in students the skills, attitudes and behaviours that will enable them to flourish in tomorrow's constantly and deeply changing world. Conventional teaching methods, which consist in the mechanical transmittal of factual knowledge and routine skills, are inadequate in this regard. Such methods must be replaced by a more dynamic teaching approach in which learning corresponds to "an active social process in which students build their own knowledge from experience." (**NCTM 1993, p. 37**) Upstream from teaching, changes can be anticipated in curricula; these will have to be enriched, without overloading them, by centering knowledge around fertile, relevant and meaningful integrating themes that are more likely to lead to targeted learning.

If the changes required in education are to produce the anticipated results, assessment practices must develop in the desired direction. Today, assessment still focuses to a large extent on measuring factual knowledge and checking routine skills. Learning associated with more elaborate processes, such as problem solving or the scientific process, more often than not is assessed via conventional methods (written tests, multiple-choice questions) that greatly limit the scope of that assessment. The following paragraphs explore possible avenues whereby assessment might contribute to the new approach to education.

Assessment must seek to present a **complete picture** of the targeted learning. All areas (knowledge, skills and behaviour) must be dealt with in the proportions determined by their actual importance in the curricula, and not on the basis of external criteria such as the ease with which they can be assessed. Moreover, assessment must be based on **clear standards, expressed in terms of learning to be achieved**, instead of in reference to given producers of statistical comparisons between groups or individuals.

Assessment must stem from **planning** which, among other things, identifies the **responsibilities of the various stakeholders** (province, school board, school, teacher and student) and guarantees the **consistency and equity of actions**. For example, external measures must complement and be in harmony with the types of assessment advocated in class, not contradict them. Assessment planning must also **equip stakeholders** by giving them indications on the relative importance of curriculum contents, appropriate means of assessing them and the criteria for doing so.

The **teacher plays a vital role** in the assessment of learning, which is built up over relatively long periods and requires ongoing monitoring as well as appropriate and timely interventions. Because of their close and constant presence, teachers are the best-placed education stakeholders to observe progress and judge the quality of such learning. Efforts should be made to facilitate assessment by teachers and improve their skills in the development and use of various measurement tools.

Students must be made aware of their responsibilities with regard to assessment. They must be informed of expectations and be able to refer to them at any time; they must be able to position themselves in relation to these expectations. Students who are able to take stock of their progress are more likely to believe in their training. Assessment by students contributes to a better understanding of the subject and develops tolerance for the views of others. Training students to engage in self-assessment, to reflect upon the quality of their work and seek to improve upon it constitutes one of the best service that the school can provide.

Assessment must contribute to **enhancing students' commitment to their studies and developing positive attitudes**, such as self-confidence and the desire to learn. Accordingly, assessment tasks must be stimulating, present a certain challenge to the student, and correspond to the student's tastes and interests. Such tasks must also be authentic and lead to useful results, raise new questions, offer a wealth of possibilities, and permit divergence, diversity, innovation and excellence.

Assessment results must be drawn from **a variety of specialized sources**. Several methods, grouped under the heading "alternative assessment measures," are proposed to facilitate the assessment of complex learning. These include formal and informal observation, questioning, interviewing, complex productions (ranging from open questions to sophisticated projects), the logbook and the portfolio. These methods, which are more difficult to apply but are also better tailored than conventional methods to the new approach to education, have not yet come into widespread use.

The purpose of assessment must not be only to measure and judge; it must also help to **improve learning**. Assessment must be an **ongoing concern** in education. This does not mean that it should take up all of one's time, but rather that one must remain alert in order to detect opportunities for and signs of progress in students. Formal assessment periods can even constitute excellent learning situations. Among the **reference frameworks** for judging learning, it is important to choose those that are most favourable to progress. **Assessment reports and** results must be expressed in **concrete terms that are understandable** to students and to their other intended readers. A balance sheet, in the form of a profile, is more likely to be useful for the subsequent monitoring of events than an overall numerical mark delivered without any other form of explanation.

Technology development should open some promising vistas in the teaching and assessment of science and mathematics. **Virtual reality** will make available a multitude of "concrete" realities offering a wealth of learning opportunities that are liable to interest students. **Hypermedia documentation** systems are already making available to students a huge quantity of visual and sound information that they can explore and discover at their own pace. **Expert learning-assessment systems** keep a memory record of the individual student's progress, analyse his/her actions and tailor the next stages to achieve optimum learning. A student who is called upon to establish a **relational data base** as part of research project will have to define the nature and structure of the sought-after information, gather that information, determine the unifying links between its various components, and program the whole thing with a view to simple and effective use. Technology can also benefit **assessment management**. The simplification of **data input procedures** (voice recognition, electronic pens, remote data entry, etc.) and the **more widespread use of data bases** will encourage the use of assessment methods that produce large amounts of data (e.g. observation checklists). Finally, we are not all that far away from the day when parents will be able to consult their child's academic record via **interactive television**. This record will be an animated version of the present descriptive report card and, among other things, will include annotated samples of the child's work as well as short filmed sequences of the child's behaviour in class.

Conclusion

New practices in assessment as in other areas require strong leadership from ministries of education. In Canada, the Council of Ministers of Education, Canada (of the provinces) has organized the School Achievement indicators Project (SAIP) to enable the assessment of math, language and science skills of students across the country. However, many of the characteristics of good assessment practice described in this paper cannot be implemented on a nationwide basis, but at the level of individual classrooms. Ensuring that these changes take place in a relatively decentralized education system is the challenge that faces Canadians now. Encouragement and support of individual teachers is the key to improvement and the Commission can assist in bringing such innovations to the general attention of teachers throughout the world.

Further Readings

Culotta, E. "Curriculum Reform : Project 2061 Offers a Benchmark." *Science*, 262, October 1993.

Corporate Higher Education Forum. *Learning Goals for K-12 Education: To Be Our Best.* Montreal, 1992, 9 pages.

NCTM (Assessment Standards Working Groups of National Council of Teachers of Mathematics). *Assessment Standards for School Mathematics* (working draft). Reston, VA, 1993, 244 pages.

NCTM (National Council of Teachers of Mathematics), *Mathematics Assessment : Myths, Models Good Questions and Practical Suggestions.* Edited by J.K. Steinmark. Reston, VA, 1991, 65 pages.

Equity Principles in the Assessment of School Learning in Canada (translation of French title), Edmonton, Alberta: Education Building North, University of Alberta, Edmonton, Alberta, T6G 2G5)

Steinmark, J.K. Assessment Alternatives in Mathematics : An overview of assessment techniques that promote learning. Sponsored by the Equals Program and the Assessment Committee of the California Mathematics Council Campaign for Mathematics. University of California, 1989, 35 pages.

Webb, N.L. Assessment of Students' Knowledge of Mathematics : Steps Toward a Theory, *Handbook of Research on Mathematics Teaching and Learning : A Project of the National Council of Teachers of Mathematics.* Edited by Douglas A. Grouws, Macmillan Publishing Company, 1992, pp 661-683.

Mr. Denis Savard
Research Officer
Conseil superieur de l education
(Sub-Commission on Natural Sceinces
Canadian Commission for UNESCO
350 Albert-Box 1047
Ottawa, Ontario - Canada K1P 5V8)

(Source: International Commission on Education for the Twenty First Centurv)

25

Information and Communication Technologies in Science and Mathematics Education

— *Milton McClaren*

Introduction

Many forms of work and services have been revolutionized by the development and application of information and communication technologies (ICT). Since the first appearance of computers in large universities and government agencies some educators have been interested in the application of ICT to the problems of instruction. Many of the first uses of computer aided instruction were developed with science and mathematics as curriculum foci. As powerful, easy to use desktop microcomputers and network infrastructures connecting widely distributed users have become generally available in schools, colleges and universities, interest in the educational potential of ICT has grown rapidly. However, as great as the potential of applying this technology in educational settings seems to be, the reality of its use in schools has lagged for behind. In Canada, many provinces have made progress in increasing the availability of computers and software in schools and in creating wide area networks to connect schools and provide them with access to a suite of information services, learning resources, and to the Internet. Students need to appreciate the power and potential of information technology as well as its limits and dangers. The curriculum in science and technology is a natural place to explore ICT, to develop understanding of it, and to apply it to the learning of science concepts and process. However, for this to happen there must be a clear appreciation by teachers, school administrators, and students of the roles which the technology should play in science programmes.

As a first step in appreciating the roles of ICT in science curriculum it may be helpful to distinguish between learning **about**, learning **with**, and learning **from** information technologies. Any contemporary programme in science education will be sorely lacking if it does not include learning about information technologies as a purpose. Students need to develop an appreciation and awareness of the potential power and application of information technologies in fields like health, recreation, government, law, science and engineering, media production and journalism, business, the fine arts, law enforcement and education. The students who are currently enrolled in school science programmes will be challenged to find or create jobs in a global economy based as much on information resources as on goods and raw materials. For the developed countries of the world, like Canada, future prosperity depends on the development of knowledge capital, and on having a work force which has sufficient understanding of ICT to be able to invent new products and services based on them. For the lesser developed countries, ICT, properly applied, offers the potential to avoid many of the problems encountered by the developed nations during the process of industrialization, including environmental degradation and the waste of raw materials and resources. Science curriculum, therefore needs to provide all students, whether they are bound for college and university science programmes or not, with an opportunity to learn about these technologies. What better way to accomplish this than by learning about science through the active use of ICT.

In many schools, computers and other information and communication technologies are still used largely as glorified typewriters, applied mainly as word processors. While a large amount of so-called educational software has been developed, a great deal of it is little more than an electronic form of drill and practice worksheets. However, there are now powerful software applications available, including symbolic manipulators like *Mathematica* ® (a software product of Wolfarm Research, Inc., 100 Trade Centre Drive, Champaign, IL.) which have the potential to change the way subjects like mathematics are taught and to call into question what is taught as well. The advent of microcomputers with expanded high speed processing capacities makes it easy to integrate audio, motion video, graphics, and text media and to provide convenient real time access to remote resources. But in many classrooms the predominant media of science instruction are still the voice of teacher, the chalkboard, text books, and the students' notes. Even conventional school libraries may form only a small part of the spectrum of information used by students. There is a real need to create science curriculum in which ICT form not only an important content element but also pay an integral role as a means of providing learning experiences and extending the available resources of the classroom and school.

But what about learning science from information and communication technologies? People sometimes speak of a knowledge explosion. There is a different among data, information, knowledge and understanding. Science curricula are often overwhelmed by the torrent of information generated by modern scientific inquiry. The Constructivist paradigm of learning and curriculum development suggests that students must develop knowledge by doing intellectual work in order to make sense of data and information. Content coverage is a poor substitute for effective and durable understanding. ICT offers a chance for school science programmes to provide students with up to date information about science and technology, with tools for the management, organization and access of information, and with tools for the simulation and modelling of science processes and principles. While there is great interest now in Personal Digital Assistants (PDA's) * to support various business operations, the development of Personal Learning Assistant might powerfully enable the work of being a student. Research also suggests that the availability of computer based electronic conferences which bring students into direct contact with on-line mentors and experts changes the traditional relationships between classroom teachers and students making the teacher a facilitator and guide to learning, rather than a living library of information. Recent developments in multimedia computing present opportunities to create highly engaging learning situations which could help students perform and understand scientific inquiry. But, the same technologies could also become highly sophisticated and expensive forms of the traditional science textbook, presenting an even more burdensome load of information to be covered by students and teachers alike.

* PDA's or Personal Digital Assistants are a new generation of small, hand held computer and communication tools. They typically feature a small screen which can be written on directly with a stylus, and built in handwriting recognition software. They are currently being placed on the market by a number of corporations which manufacture computers or electronic equipment. The PLA does not yet exist as such.

Conclusion

The challenge presented to science education by ICT is to find a way of incorporating the technologies as integral components both of the agenda for instruction and of the learning environment while using them to enliven and improve the nature of science programmes in schools. Unless this is done, ICT will either continue to be, as they largely are now, extraneous or peripheral to the regular and traditional patterns of school operations, or they will emerge as highly expensive and sophisticated electronic textbooks disempowering both teachers and students in the learning process. On a global scale it will be important to help create greater equity between greater and lesser developed nations in terms of access to ICT and to the world of on-line resources made available through international wide area networks. Unless this is done, the advent of information and communication technologies will simply widen the gap between have and have-not nations.

Further Reading

Alessi, Stephen M. & Stanely R. Trollip (1991.) *Computer based Instruction.* (Second Ed.) Englewood Cliffs (NJ) : Prentice Hall.

Apple, Michael W. (1985) *Making Knowledge Legitimate : Power, Profit and the Textbook, in* : Current Thought on Curriculum. Molnar, A. (Ed.) Alexandria (VA) : Association for Supervision and Curriculum Development.

Brand, Steward (1987). *The Media Lab. Markham* (ON) : Penguin, Canada.

Brooks, Jacqueline and Martin G. (1993). *In Search of Understanding.* The Case for Constructivist Classrooms. Alexandria (VA) : Association for Supervision and Curriculum Development.

Education Technology Centre of British Columbia. (1990). *International Perspectives : Education and Technology.* Proceedings of the ITEC Conference, October 24, 1990. Collis, B. and Mussion. J. (eds.) Sidney (B.C.) : The Education Technology Centre of B.C.

Goodlad, John I. (1984). *A Place Called School.* N.Y. : MCGraw Hill.

Inventing Our Future : An Action Plan for Canada's Prosperity, Steering Group on Prosperity, Ottawa, 1992

Mc Claren, Milton (1988), *A Curricular Perspective on the Principle of Understanding. in* : Marx, R.W. (Ed.) Curriculum : Towards Developing a Common Understanding. Victoria (BC) : Ministry of Education.

McMahen, Chris. (1992). *The Design and Implementation of the CMC Project "Salmonids on Line"*. Unpublished M.Ed Project. Burnaby (B.C.) : Simon Fraser University.

Mustard, J. Fraser. (1994) *The Great Reckoners. Acumen.* February/March, 1994. pps. 20-26.

Roszak, Theodore. (1986) *The Cult of Information.* N.Y. : Pantheon.

Shaiken, Harlye. (1985) *Work Transformed.* Automation and Labour in the Computer Age. N.Y. : Holt, Rinehart & Winston.

Dr. Milton McClaren,
Director,
Field Services and Teacher In-Service Education
Faculty of Education
Simon Fraser University
Burnaby (B.C.)
Canada V5A 1S6

(Source: International Commission on Education for the Twenty First Century)

26

The Participation of Girls and Young Women in Science and Mathematics Education

— *Monique Frize and Jane Mcginn-Giberson*

Introduction

Barriers still discourage many young women from enrolling in physics, chemistry, and advanced mathematics at the secondary school level, thus pre-empting their choice of post-secondary programs in science and engineering. The enrolment of women in Canadian undergraduate engineering programs increased from 12 per cent to just under 20 per cent between 1989 and 1993. The number of women graduate students and faculty also remains dismally low and have not followed gains at the undergraduate levels. Other professions such as medicine, law, dentistry, and veterinary medicine have reached and maintained gender - balanced enrolments for some time. The points clearly to the existence of subtle barriers in engineering and physical science programs. The climate, culture, teaching styles and curricula must all be modified in ways that integrate women's needs if these barriers are to be removed.

Systemic barriers at the secondary school level include :

- Cultural influences and gender-role stereotyping at home and at school;

- The lack of women role models as teachers and in textbooks;
- Teaching styles; studies have shown that only 5 percent of the population has a "mentally centered" learning style, yet most science, mathematics and engineering teaching is done in that style, while 85 per cent of both women and men prefer a relationally centered style;
- Misperceptions that many non-traditional occupations are for men only; many parents, teachers and career counsellors place more important on and greater expectations for the career plans of boys than for those of girls and show more concern for the overall performance of boys;
- Physical appearance rather than a good education are emphasized for girls in popular and teen culture;
- Erosion of self-esteem in girls between the age of thirteen and seventeen affects their performance and choices;
- The message that "brains and femininity are incompatible" may come from boys, parents, other girls, and some educators;
- School board policies, expectations of universities and attitudes of employers may also be a problem.

At the university level also, sexist bias exists and appears in various forms:

- women are consistently under represented in textbooks; examples and references relate to masculine interests, women and men are depicted in stereotypical roles;
- There are few women faculty available as role models;
- Most courses are taught with a narrow focus on particular topics, without links to broader societal realities;
- Myths based on a masculine view of excellence -

concerning merit, awards and appointments and also the value of intellectual work and success in seeking funding and recognition - are prejudicial to women's success and to their integration into these fields;

- With regard to course content, " a prevalent attitude is that the presence of emotional, personal issues and feelings... indicates the absence of academic and intellectual content."

Current endeavors to combat sexism in science and mathematics classroom include :

- Education faculties sensitizing future teachers about systemic sexism in the classroom;
- Workshops with parents and career counsellors to encourage them to be a positive influence, to avoid stereotyping and to challenge girls as much as boys to develop their full potential;
- Some schools (teachers) select textbooks which do not portray women and men in traditional stereotyped roles, books that include profiles of women scientists, engineers, mathematicians; (here, the province of Quebec is a good example);
- Some province have achieved an equal representation of women in mathematics and sciences classes at the secondary level; (Quebec and Saskatchewan are good examples);
- Some schools are using a cooperative learning environment in classes, others have adopted a single sex approach, or a content and teaching style that incorporates the experiences and interests of girls;
- Videos have been produced on careers in engineering and science, showing how engineers and scientists apply their knowledge to the benefit of humankind, to solve problems, and to design the world we live and work in; such videos make these careers more visible and

appealing to young women;

- Mentor programs, where young women students meet women in non-traditional occupations, create a long term support needed to eliminate the barriers.

At the post secondary level much is also needed to change the climate and culture for women:

- Universities should encourage the use of gender inclusive language and the creation of a non-threatening environment in the classroom—teaching assessment questionnaires should ask students about this aspect in each class;
- Universities could distribute a booklet on gender-inclusive language to each instructor and provide gender sensitivity training to faculty, staff and graduate assistants;
- Faculties should track students on academic probation and develop a mentor program, especially for students in minority groups;
- Special efforts should be made to attract and fund women students in graduate programs; they form the pool for future women faculty;
- Studies are needed to identify gender differences in graduate student funding, and the quality of relationships with supervisors;
- Women faculty need to be proactively sought and hired. Objective hiring criteria would be based on the availability of women in the pool of graduates— it is frequent to observe that even where affirmative action policies exist, the policy is often ignored or given lip service;
- Caplan's meritocracy myth must be exposed and attitudes changed on how excellence is defined.

The use of cooperative learning and teaching style

creates a positive environment and team work with which women are comfortable;—it has also been shown to be far more effective than the traditional method for both women and men students alike. In addition, relating topics to societal realities would be most effective. The curriculum should develop multidisciplinary topics that are related to the quality of the environment and the quality of life; examples are : biophysics, environmental engineering, biomedical engineering, water resources engineering, biological engineering, etc. Such programs in Canada have achieved gender-balanced enrolments. In contrast, topics which are narrowly-focussed and classical in their approach find the lowest enrolment of women. When these courses are 'humanized' with some societal context, they will certainly be attended by greater numbers of women.

Conclusion

The current 'culture of science' originates from the middle-ages and from the industrial revolution. One of the negative aspects of this culture passed down from these early times is 'man's domination and control of nature, of the planet and of its natural resources'. This image has deterred many talented women and men from considering the study of science. The perception (or reality) of a masculine culture in science creates a systemic barrier for many women. But their absence deprives these fields of an enriching perspective. Strategies must be sought to successfully eradicate sexism and harassment in our universities. Aspects of the current culture that make some women feel uncomfortable must be identified and ways sought to integrate and value feminine perspectives, especially in the creation of new scholarly work.

Further Reading

Brooks C. (1986) "Instructor's Handbook : Working with Female Relational Learners in Technology and Trades Training." Fanshawe College and Ontario Ministry of Skills Development, Toronto, Canada.

Caplan, P. (1992) "Lifting a Ton of Feathers. A Women's Guide a Surviving in the Academic World". (A project of the Council of Ontario Universities Committee on the Status of Women), University of Toronto Press, Toronto, Canada.

CCWE (1992) "More than Just Numbers". Report of the Canadian Committee on Women in Engineering. Copies can be obtained from M. Frize, UNB, Fredericton, NB, E3B 5A3.

Frize M., McGinn-Giberson, J., Shelton, C. (1992) "Engineering Design Tomorrow's World". VHS Video, 22 min., Northern Telecom-NSERC Women in Engineering Chair, UNB, Frederiction, NB, Canada E3B 5A3.

Noble D.F.(1992) "A world Without Women". Technology Review, May-June: 52-60.

Ontario Women's Directorate (1993) " Words that Count Women In" 2 Carlton St., 12th floor, Toronto, Ontario M5B 2M9.

Peltz W.H. (1992)" Can Girls + Science - Stereotypes = Success? Subtle Sexism in Science Studies". The Science Teacher, December : 44-49.

Tobias S. (1990) "They're not dumb, they're different". Research Corporation, 6840 East Broadway Boulevard, Tucson, Arizona 85710-2815.

Dr. Monique Frize - *Univerity of New Brunswick*
and
Ms Jane Mcginn-Giberson
Sub-Commission on Natural Sciences
Canadian Commission for UNESCO
Box 1047 Ottawa K1P 5V8-Canada

(Source: International Commission on Education for the Twenty First Century)

27

New Directions in Science and Technology Education in Alberta

— Alberta Education

Over the past three to four years, the province of Alberta has been extensively revising its science programme for secondary students (ages 12 to 18). The programme content is new and different; as well, Alberta has pursued some new and different routes with regard to the curriculum development and implementation processes.

Purpose of New Programme. An Alberta Education vision paper published in 1990 includes this statement about science education : "Our students must have strong backgrounds in science, be more enthusiastic about careers in science, and be able to use science and technology to understand and improve society and the world."

One goal of the recent revision was to develop a science programme that will meet the needs of all students. As we approach the 21st century, it is abundantly clear that every citizen must have a certain degree of scientific literacy. At the same time, it is more important than ever before to have a highly skilled scientific community, and the education of future scientists begins during the years of basic education. Therefore, Alberta's new science programme ensures that : (a) All students graduating from Alberta schools will be well prepared to work and live successfully in our highly scientific and technological society, and (b) students who plan to pursue specialized careers in science (e.g., medicine, biochemistry, engineering) will have opportunities to acquire the advanced knowledge, skills and attitudes they require in order to achieve their goals.

As well, the new programme shifts the focus of science education in several ways : (a) the Science, Technology and Society (STS) concept is integrated into all courses (students learn to understand the tremendous impact of science and technology on society by applying their "pure science" knowledge to societal issues;) (b) students have more opportunities to understand the "big ideas" of science and see science as a unified body of knowledge. At the same time, those who choose to do so are able to specialize in the specific scientific disciplines of physics, biology and chemistry (in senior high school, ages 15 to 18); (c) students are more actively engaged in "doing science". They learn that science is a human, hands-on activity; (d) students learn more about the scientific world view, about the processes of scientific inquiry and enterprise and about careers in science.

Structures of New Programme. A common programme is offered for students at grade levels one through ten. An extension to this common programme is provided for in the eleventh and twelfth years of schooling, so students have the opportunity to specialize in one or more of the sciences.

At the junior high level, the programme takes the form of 18 units, each of which focuses on a specific area of knowledge. Each unit also conveys an understanding of the following aspects of science:

- nine units develop an understanding of the nature of science;
- six units examine the relationship of science and technology;
- three units examine the role of science in a social context.

As described in the previous section, the senior high programme strives to meet the needs of individual students. The majority of students (approximately 80%) take Science 10 in their first year of senior high school. Science 10 is an integrated but rigorously academic introductory course. (Alberta high schools also offer two other high school science routes for students who are having difficulty learning : Science 14-24 and Science 16-26).

In the following two year (after Science 10), some students choose to pursue as many as three specific science disciplines (Biology 20-30, Chemistry 20-30 and Physics 20-30). Others choose one or two of these specific routes, along with Science 20 and 30, which are also integrated but academically rigorous courses. Some (those who do not plan to major in science in post-secondary studies) chooses to do only Science 10-20-30. A few move from Science 10 to Science 24 (a less academic course) and do not take science at all in their last year of high school.

Curriculum development and implementation processes. A broader range of people was involved in developing the new science curriculum: over 60 professional, business and parent groups helped educators review and provide direction for programmes, resources and teacher in-service programmes.

The development process included customized texts for junior high courses and for Science 10-20-30, and the development of test item banks to help teachers effectively evaluate students' success in acquiring the expected concepts, skills and attitudes. A new part of the programme, called "Assessment Standards", is being developed to provide guidance for assessment of students both at the school and provincial level. These standards will be used in the design of provincial school-leaving examinations and will set clear provincial standards for each grade level, across the different science courses. Distance education materials are also being developed for the new courses.

The three universities in Alberta (with faculties of

science and education working together) have been partners with Alberta Education in providing in-service sessions for teachers of the new science programmes. These sessions have been highly successful. These in-service initiatives, in combination with an active communications programme which includes one-day information sessions being held around the province and videos for teachers, have helped teachers to prepare for the implementation of the new science directions.

One other important aspect of implementation is the involvement of a large network of community resource persons — scientists, people in business and industry, and others. These people support the science programme in a variety of ways: for example, visiting classrooms to share their knowledge and interest in science with students, offering summer workshops for teachers and students, or providing funding, scholarships or equipment.

Conclusions

Initial monitoring reports on the junior high courses, which have been offered since 1990-1991 are that : ■A majority of students like the programme and the textbooks; feel that science is relevant, useful, interesting and fun; believe they learn more fro hands-on activities. ■A majority of teachers say the programme is enjoyable and useful, and appropriate for the students' interests and abilities. ■Some teachers feel a need for updated facilities and materials, and more time for science instruction. ■On the science portion of the 1990-91 International Assessment of Educational Progress (IAEP) II Study. Alberta's 13-year old students ranked first in Canada and third internationally.

The 30-level portion of the new senior high programmes are still undergoing field validation. The results are generally positive. Some further revisions are necessary, mainly to make expected outcomes and some standards clearer. There are still some concerns in the field, such as teaching science to students who lack adequate mathematical skills, getting students to become more independent learners, helping students decide which courses to select and providing clear information about the post-secondary programmes that students can pursue if they complete Science 20-30. Alberta Education staff are working to overcome these challenges.

Alberta Education
Devonian Building, West Tower
11160 Jasper Avenue
Edmonton, Alberta
Canada T5K OL2

(Source: International Commission on Education for the Twenty First Century)

28

The Education of Science and Mathematics Teachers

,—Tom Russel

Introduction

The education of science and mathematics teachers comprises both their education in science and/or mathematics and their education as teachers of these disciplines. The first of these, while obviously essential to good teaching, does not necessarily provide for an easy acquisition of the second. To a considerable extent, and more than many other school subjects (3), Science and mathematics are "right answer" disciplines typically driven more by memory and tight logic than by first-hand experience and experimentation. In sharp contrast, learning to teach is an intensely personal experience driven by technique and a rhetoric of practices devoid of well-articulated rationales. This contrast between learning one's discipline and learning to teach can be acutely uncomfortable for teachers of science and mathematics. If it is not understood and resolved during teacher education, then a restricted teaching career can result. The present "Brief" will deal principally with the `learning to teach' aspects of the education of science and mathematics teachers.

Both teaching and teacher education are shaped profoundly by traditions of practical routines that long ago became disconnected from their original justifications. Our common sense world of everyday conversation assumes, quite erroneously, that learning from experience is an automatic, transparent, and self-evident process. Just as it is incorrect to see learning as a process that is complete as a result of "being told", so it is also incorrect and misleading to assume that learning is complete after "having an experience"—whether one is a science student doing "hands-on experiments," a beginning teacher in a practice teaching assignment, or an experienced science teacher tackling a persistent dilemma of classroom practice.

Major developments in research in mathematics and science education and in teacher education since 1980 are only gradually having an impact at the level of practice in our schools and our programs of teacher education. Central to the developments described below is the *questioning of epistemological assumptions embedded in traditional educational practices* at all levels of schooling.

The "Project for Enhancing Effective Learning" (PEEL), which began in 1985 in Melbouren, Australia, is an outstanding illustration of a range of similar but less well documented innovations in teaching. The project's primary aim is to "foster student's independent learning through training for enhanced metacognition" (2, p. iii; the term" metacognition" refers to an individuals' knowledge about, awareness of, and control of learning). The project also aims to "change teacher's attitudes and behaviours to ones that promote such learning," "Investigate processes of teacher and student change," and "identify factors that influence successful implementation of a program to improve the quality of classroom learning".

Overall, the PEEL project seeks to foster "quality learning'—an aim that appeals to virtually all teachers, but one that has traditionally eluded their grasp. One strategy involves identifying students' "poor learning tendencies" and recognizing that many passive student behaviours occur as responses to traditional teaching behaviours. The project has gone on to identify teaching strategies that foster observable "good learning behaviours" by students. Teachers and students alike found the experience of change overwhelming at times (1), yet the goal carried them along. The project's conclusions are particularly relevant to the teaching of mathematics and science : Change is possible, but it requires time, effort, collaboration, openness, support, self-criticism and a focus on the classroom.

The strategies and conclusions of the PEEL project have had their counterparts in Canada (6, 7) and elsewhere. It is important to realize that the challenges to science teaching posed by the Australian teachers and researchers have direct parallels as **challenges to improve the education of teachers** of mathematics and science. Participation by teachers and teacher educators in genuine rethinking of practices demands considerable self-reflection and analysis. While "reflection" has long been an element of teacher preparation, Schon's (9) argument that "reflection-in-action" is a critical process in the development of professional knowledge renewed our attention to that domain of teacher development. While "reflective practice" is now a familiar term in teacher education, finding ways to foster reflective practice in teacher preparation may prove even more challenging for teacher educators than for teachers.

The development of interest in the quality of learning has occurred simultaneously with research into the process by which students learn, particularly with reference to the nature of scientific concepts. This research is often associated with the term "constructivism"—another board term with multiple interpretations. A constructivist perspective holds that learning is a personal and active process of making meaning, not the simple transmission of words from person to person. There is growing recognition within science education the students of science do not relate laboratory experiences directly or easily to the science concepts that the experiences are meant to illustrate or stimulate thought about. When Edwards and Mercer studied children learning first-hand about the behaviour of pendula, they concluded that experience often leads to ritual knowledge rather than the desired understanding of principles. Similarly, experiences of teaching-in a practicum or throughout one's career—are not directly or easily related to one's personal beliefs and assumptions about how students learn and why one teaches as one does. If our programs of preservice and in service teacher education fail to challenge the everyday assumption that action follows from and is consistent with one's beliefs, then teachers will continue to develop ritualized practices. Research at Queen's University is exploring this cluster of issues in the context of the preparation of physics teachers.

Conclusion

Changes in the *preparation* of science and mathematics teachers come no more easily than do changes in the *teaching* of science and mathematics. New perspective such as those described above point the way to important new possibilities in an era when schools and teacher education programs are subject to growing criticisms for failing to meet society's expectations. Projects based in schools have shown more progress than those based in teacher education programs. Some teacher educators are realizing that they must apply new perspective to personal practices before advocating them to others, and this is a promising first step.

New perspectives do not lead directly to defensible new practices, just as learning from experience is not automatic. There are essential processes of critical judgement involved in assuring society that we have improved our educative enterprises. All teachers begin with the values implicit in their personal experiences of school and in the disciplines they have studied. New practices must be mediated in terms of the disciplines we teach, by deliberations within relevant professional communities. These include communities of teachers within schools and universities and the community of experienced teachers who observe and guide the earliest experiences of beginning teachers. It is within these communities that new partnerships must be formed to pursue collectively the development of improved practices of teaching and teacher education in science and mathematics.

Further Reading

Baird, J., & Mitchell, I. (1986). *Improving the quality of teaching and learning: An Australian Case Study-- The PEEL Project.* Melboure : Monash University Press.

Baird, J. & Northfield, J. (1992). *Learning from the PEEL Experience.* Melboure : Monash University Press.

Barnes, D. (1976). *From communication to curriculum.* Harmondsworth : Penguin.

Driver, R. (1983). *The pupil as scientist?* Milton Keynes : Open University Press.

Edwards, D., & Mercer, N. (1987). *Common knowledge : The development of understanding in the classroom.* London : Routledge.

Erickson, G.L., & MacKinnon, A.M. (1991). Seeing classrooms in new ways : On becoming a science teacher. In D.A. Schon (Ed.) *The reflective turn* (pp. 15-36). New York : Teachers College Press.

Nadeau, R., & Desautels, J. (1984). *Epistemology and the teaching of science.* Toronto : University of Toronto Guidance Centre.

Munby, H. & Russell, T. (1994). The authority of experience in learning to teach : Messages from a physics methods class. *Journal of Teacher Education,* vol. 45, pp. 86-95.

Schon, D.A. (1983). *The reflective practitioner : How professionals think in action.* New York : Basic Books.

Tobin, K. (1993). *The practice of constructivism in science education.* Washington, DC : AAAS Press.

Whitehead, J. (1993). T*he growth of educational knowledge : Creating your own living educational theories*. Bornemouth, England : Hyde Publications.

Dr. Tom Russell
Faculty of Education
Queen's University Sciences
MacArthur Hall
Kingston (Ontario)
Canada K7L 3N6

(Source: International Commission on Education for the Twenty First Century)

29

The ILO/UNESCO Recommendation Concerning the Status of Teachers, 1996

— Bill Ratteree

Introduction

The Recommendation concerning the Status of Teachers was adopted by a special intergovernmental conference convened by UNESCO in cooperation with the ILO in 1966. It evolved out of 20 years of concern and numerous expert and interagency meetings of the ILO and UNESCO, involving representatives of Governments and the teaching profession.

The extent of progress in realizing the application of the Recommendation's provisions has been monitored since 1968 by a joint ILO/UNESCO Committee of Experts which meets every three years.

The Recommendation is not legally binding. It is a set of guidelines for good practice in adopting policy, plans, legislation, administrative rules, mechanisms for decision-making etc. It is comprised of a preamble and 146 operative paragraphs, divided into 13 sections which relates to the most important professional, material and social concerns of teachers. These are summarized below.

The **definitions** and **scope** specify that the

Recommendation applies to all those persons in public and private schools who are responsible for pupils' education from nursery through secondary levels, including technical, vocational and art education. It does not apply to post-secondary institutions. Their status means the standing or appreciation of teachers derived both from their function and professional competence, and their remuneration and working conditions.

In its **guiding principles**, the Recommendation emphasizes that educational advancement is largely dependent on the qualifications and ability of teaching staff. A proper status for teachers as professionally and due regard for teaching as a profession are of major importance for educational aims and objectives. Teacher's organizations should be recognized as a force for educational advance and should therefore be associated with determining educational policy.

Education objectives and policies should repose on a foundation of a State-organized and funded network of schools, sufficient in quantity and quality, without prejudice to the liberty of parents to choose for their children, nor for individuals and bodies to establish and direct, educational institutions other than State established schools. There should be close cooperation between competent authorities, teachers' organizations, organizations of employers and workers, parents and other interested parties in education to define its policy and objectives.

The Recommendation contains detailed guidelines on **preparation for the profession,** which address the policies determining selection for entry into teacher preparation programmes, the structure and content of such programmes and the role of teacher-preparation institutions. Additional guidelines on **further education for teachers** stress the importance of in-service and further education of teachers to enable them to improve their qualifications, alter or enlarge the scope of their work, seek promotion and keeup to date with the content and methods of their subjects. Authorities should promote a wide system of free and continuing education for teachers, in consultation with teacher's organizations.

The Recommendation's provisions naturally refer to *employment and career*, specifying at the beginning that policy governing entry into the teaching profession, and rules naturally refer to *employment and career*, specifying at the beginning that policy governing entry into the teaching profession, and rules laying down teachers' obligations and rights, should be clearly defined in collaboration with teachers' organizations. Advancement and promotion structures should allow for flexible movement of teachers between levels of education, recognition of additional responsibilities, experience and objective assessment based on strictly professional criteria. Security of tenure is an essential element of stability for the individual teacher and education, reinforced by clearly defined and transparent disciplinary procedures. The Recommendation also contains detailed provisions to encourage women teachers with family responsibilities to remain in or return to the teaching profession, as well as the value and conditions under which part-time teaching service should be organized.

A very important section **on the rights and responsibilities of teachers** deals first and foremost with the delicate question of professional freedom, emphasizing the concept of academic freedom within the teaching profession based on the participation of teachers and their organizations in the development of curricula, choice of teaching methods and fair assessment techniques for pupils. The responsibilities of teachers and their organizations include defining and maintaining high professional standards and the establishment of codes of ethics or conduct. Considerable emphasis is placed on consultation with teachers organizations on improvements in educational quality. Respect for the rights of teachers includes teachers civic rights, the importance of negotiations over salaries and working conditions, the establishment of dispute settlement mechanisms and the right of teachers' organizations to take steps open to other organizations to defend their interests.

Nearly thirty provisions of the Recommendation speak to the **condition for effective teaching and learning.** The most important refer to class size- permitting individual attention for pupils - and hours of work, which should be established in consultation with teachers' organizations and include all factors of teacher's work classroom teaching, preparation of lessons, evaluation of pupils, extra-curricular and supervisory duties and consultations with parents. Other provisions concern leave arrangements, teacher exchanges and safety constructed and adequately maintained school buildings. A section of the Recommendation suggests measures such as housing, travel facilities and special hardship allowances to encourage teachers to work in rural or remote areas.

Teachers' salaries figure prominently among the Recommendation's concerns, based on the principle that these should reflect the importance of the teaching function and responsibilities to society. Salaries should therefore compare favourably with salaries paid to occupations with equivalent qualifications and take account of differences in qualifications, experience and responsibilities of different teaching posts. The Recommendation's guidelines on salary structure, with scales established in agreement with teacher's organizations, are set out in a way that helps to avoid injustices or anomalies that might serve as a disincentive among groups of teachers. It does not advocate merit pay systems unless these are agreed upon with the teachers' organizations.

Another 15 provisions concern teachers' **social security,** based on international labour standards, which should cover medical care, sickness, employment injury, old-age invalidity and survivors, benefits, as well as the mean of providing coverage. A final section of the Recommendation suggests ways in which teacher **shortages** can be overcome in the interest of educational quality.

Mr. Bill Ratteree
Salaried Employees and Professional Workers branch
Sectoral Activities Department
International Labor Organization
Geneva, Switzerland

(Source: International Commission on Education for the Twenty First Century)

30

Teachers in the 21st Century: Some Observations on their Role and Status

— *Bill Ratteree*

Introduction

The future rule and status of teachers must be seen within the framework of the **central place teachers occupy in education and training.** They constitute the key elements without which organized education as now conceived in societies of the 20th century could not function. This is the basis for the set of guidelines contained in the ILO/UNESCO Recommendation concerning the Status of Teachers and the work of the Joint ILO/UNESCO Committee of Experts which has monitored and promoted the application of these guidelines since 1968. The challenge of the future is to transform a universal truth into sustained action by educational authorities which elevates teachers' material and social status to that which meets the high expectations of every society for its education system. The training for what may very well be more than 50 million teachers worldwide by the year 2000, and the compensation for their services - ranging from 50 to 80 per cent of public current educational expenditure in almost all countries, recently exceeding 90 per cent in many poorer ones—constitute an enormous actual and future investment in education. Moreover, societies are increasingly concerned with the quality of teaching and learning in schools, how to better organize educational systems to meet changing needs and therefore, what kind of teachers to train, recruit and maintain in the teaching profession.

The needs differ according to the economic, political, social and cultural factors specific to each country. They range from high-income, industrialized and service-based countries whose learning institutions increasingly stress the acquisition of knowledge and skills of a creative and problem-solving nature, to low-income, largely agriculturally based economies, whose education systems must establish the basis for acceding to a highly developed economic status by emphasizing first and foremost the acquisition of basic literacy and numeracy skills of the vast majority of the population. The challenges are daunting: building a non-exclusionary, high level educational network accessible to all; creating the basis for permanent education and training opportunities adapted to changing needs; and ensuring it all within a climate of economic and fiscal restriction.

The **implication for thé role and functions of teachers and their organizations will also vary**. These may be looked at from the standpoint of four key sets of variables ; training and career; remuneration; teaching conditions; and participation. The **first** concerns the linkage between INITIAL AND CONTINUAL TEACHER TRAINING, RECRUITMENT AND CAREER DEVELOPMENT. The consensus within the ILO is that initial training standards, which have remained high over time in most countries, should remain high in recognition of the complexity of teaching and to avoid a decline in quality. There is, however, a need to expand the continual training component to take account of changing educational needs.

For the investment in teacher preparation to be fully realized, both aspects must also be integrated into a comprehensive human resource package in education, based on an interlocking continuum of training, recruitment and career prospects which will favour a dynamic and creative schooling environment. Recruitment criteria, for example will need to favour aptitude and motivation to teach, not just the acquisition of credentials. Career structures will need to become more open, providing alternative instructional (as opposed to purely administrative) paths for highly skilled teachers, as well as opportunities for exchanges between schools and training sites and the world of work, underpinned by leave and return rights without loss of acquired benefits. Relatively simple but productive professional development techniques linked to career opportunities will have to be generalized and effectively employed. A key issue will be ensuring equality of opportunity and treatment between men and women, not the least for the positive impact that women teachers can have on girls' access to education and training. Policies and incentives will increasingly have to render family responsibilities and career advancement compatible to ensure that women are not only recruited in large numbers, but also return to the profession after interruptions for family reasons and achieve equality in position of responsibility.

A **second** set of factors affecting future teachers' functions concerns salaries and other material benefits. Available evidence indicates that, with a few exceptions in high-income countries, teacher salaries have not maintained comparability with professions requiring similar qualifications, nor have they been adjusted sufficiently for inflation in recent years. In many African countries salaries are not even paid on time. The consequences are frequently multiple, and self-perpetuating: a decline in the quality of individuals recruited into teaching; the loss of qualified and experienced teachers who are attracted to other jobs; and general disinterest in sustaining creative performance. The impact will be most dramatic in low-income countries subject to economic and fiscal restrictions, where multiple job-holding, teacher absenteeism and recourse to private teaching schemes are becoming the rule. Uncorrected, schooling in many countries will inexorably decline, as basic skills are not taught, or taught poorly, student dropout levels among low-income families will likely increase and the education system will become dysfunctional relative to its basic mission.

Ensuring salaries comparable to rates of equivalent professionals and efficient pay administration are therefore essential. It is important also to avoid lightly-conceived merit or differentiated pay schemes where they are not constructed on two solid foundations; objective and fair performance appraisal systems and the application of schemes which evaluate and reward teachers on the basis of whole school or institutional performance, rather than merely individuals. The ILO consensus is that strategies need to be formulated to establish material incentives broad enough to motivate all teachers, and to use modern management techniques to provide objective assessment of teachers work. The role of teachers' organizations in this sensitive area is vital, as set out in the 1966 ILO/UNESCO Recommendation, reaffirmed by the Joint Committee of Experts.

A **third** set of variables which go to the heart of the teachers' future role and function concerns the *Conditions for effective teaching and learning.* In other words, will the basic contours of teacher's working conditions - class size, workload and nature of the work demanded, teaching materials and the occupational health of teachers - favour or work against the realization of educational objectives ? Class size and mandatory hours of work have decreased slightly or remained stable in most high-income countries, yet the strains of teaching multi-skill and multi-ethnic classes, maintaining orderly classrooms and assuming more of the functions traditionally exercised by other institutions of society have increased. Among the resulting phenomena are greater levels of stress and teacher burnout, (as many as 25 to 33 per cent of teachers may be significantly affected), producing departures from the profession and lower, less creative performance levels. Previously excessive class sizes have reaches intolerable levels in the least developed countries, compounded by the well-documented lack of the most basic teaching materials as educational expenditures have been restricted.

Creative, problem-solving classrooms of the future based on work groups, team-teaching methodologies and new technologies, will require classes, especially those with heterogeneous student populations, that do not exceed certain levels, the primacy of the teaching function over administrative tasks, pupil behaviour and respect for teachers which do not negatively impact on professional motivation, and teamwork and support from colleagues and administrators, parents and political figures. The resources devoted to education will accordingly be crucial.

A **fourth** set of variables running like a common thread through the others is the extent to which teachers and their organizations will PARTICIPATE IN EDUCATIONAL DECISION-MAKING, THROUGH CONSULTATIONS AND COLLECTIVE BARGAINING. A worldwide trend towards decentralization of educational management has not been matched by a corresponding evolution towards greater participation of teachers and their organizations in the decision-making process. Yet, the success of future reforms will depend in no small part on the degree to which teaching professionals share in the decisions that are taken, and therefore have a stake in their successful implementation. Changing career development patterns, equitable (and acceptable) appraisal systems, differentiated salary structures, teamwork and more creative classroom organization are just some of the decision critical to the future role of teachers which will increasingly need to be made with greater involvement of teachers and their organizations.

The alternatives - confrontation or indifference, or both-tend to undermine the ultimate success of the changes. On the other hand, there is a body of evidence which suggests that substantial reforms can be made in the way teachers perform their work, and schools are organized, if mechanisms for genuine consultation on educational policy and collective bargaining on terms and conditions of employment are respected where they exist, and introduced where they do not. Guidance on this fundamental question of process is provided in the ILO/UNESCO Recommendation and in ILO standards on freedom of association and collective bargaining. Respect for the universal rights set out in these international standards is a cornerstone of a democratic society, and a linchpin in the inseparable relationship between the rights and the responsibilities to which teaching professionals should adhere in the educational systems of tomorrow.

Further Reading

ILO/UNESCO Recommendation concerning the Status of Teachers, 1966 (adopted by the Special Intergovernmental Conference on the Status of Teachers, Paris, 5 October 1966) and available from UNESCO and ILO.

Mr. Bill Ratteree
Salaried Employees and
Professional Workers Branch
Sectoral Activities Department
International Labor Organization
Geneva, Switzerland

(Source: International Commission on Education for the Twenty First Century)

31

Creating an Enlightened Citizenry: Libraries and Education

— *Marianne Scott*

Introduction

Our fundamental assumption is that the provision of public education and information is essential to fostering the informed citizenry necessary for a democratic society. In many different societies, libraries, as places for public gathering, providers of reference and information services on site and at a distance, teachers of how information and knowledge are organized and accessed, collectors of multi-media communal resources, and gateways to the collections of other libraries, find their *raison d'être* in this first principle. In upholding the principles of public access to information and in support of formal education, collective and individual, and lifelong learning on the part of all individuals, libraries are essential institutions within a democratic society.

Description - Libraries and Education : Libraries work to preserve and make accessible the intellectual content and heritage of humanity in the service of creating an enlightened citizenry. For several centuries, library development has been built upon the premises of lifelong learning and the necessity of providing access to information as a keystone of a democratic society. For many people, in a time where schooling was not universal, where higher education was the domain of elites, where any hope of personal advancement was limited to a few precious hours after work, the local library was the beacon to a better world. Generations have availed themselves of library resources in the pursuit of skills, knowledge and personal progress.

Generally speaking, educators recognize the important role libraries play in supporting and complementing the curriculum and in the learning experience of the student. Even in countries where resources are insufficient to support a large publishing sector, well-conceived donated book programmes thrive. Children are introduced to the wonders of reading and to the development to information skills through their school or public libraries. No greater evidence of the importance of the library is stronger than a visit into a children's section of a library where the joy and fascination of children in their first exploration of books are palpable.

Today's youth faces many challenges. Problems such as unemployment, social and family upheaval, abuse in many forms contribute to a seemingly bewildering environment fraught with uncertainties, social pressures and dangers. For many communities, libraries and information centres provide teenagers with a secure environment in which to find the information and advice necessary to help them find and develop their survival skills. Through books and magazines, through music and video and, increasingly, through computers and multi-media, the library provides doors to other experiences.

The centrality of the library to higher education is marked by its location on the campuses of colleges and universities around the world. There is evidence that the use of these library collections and services has increased - more users and greater use of the resources. What students, teachers and scholars could pursue meaningful research without access to the wealth of work done before them? While there is no doubt that new information and knowledge are being produced at a greater rate than in previous generations, it is also evident that understanding and mutual respect need time, a conducive environment and appropriate resources to take root.

Public libraries also serve the formal and informal demands of lifelong learning. The range of materials that libraries provide opens a vast world to individuals who may be deprived of opportunities to explore it in any other fashion. The immigrant seek to learn the language of his new land. The student read for examinations. The adult illiterate meets the tutor. The blind person is able to us adaptive technologies and to take home a talking book. The mechanic looks for instructions on the repair of machines. The small business person begins his analysis of a new business opportunity. The citizen seeks answers to legal issues related to his/her rights. While answers to some of these types of enquiry may soon be accessible from home, there are two essential realities: libraries are social institutions with trained and dedicated staff to assist users, and the collective resource is organized for browsing or systematic search.

As we move into an era of widespread electronic communication, libraries are again at the forefront of technological innovation : finding new ways of providing services, wrestling with the challenges of organizing widely distributed information, developing the standards and applications that will give meaningful access to the wealth of opportunities promised by the information explosion. In an era of widely distributed electronic resources, the skills of libraries in the intellectually - and labour intensive organization and management of information resources will prove essential.

Electronic networking among libraries provides new opportunities: the means to streamline the collection and management of resources and the ability to provide resources for distance education programmes to communities and individuals around the world. Libraries are using emerging technologies to reach out to wider constituencies and to bring information resources to bear where none were previously available. Libraries, forums for public discourse, continue this role in the new on-line environment, as they move to become centres for social computing, facilitators of access, and equitable providers of essential services and content to the new information society.

The freedom to read and to have access to information unrestricted by censorship are essential to ensuring the free-flow of ideas that is so critical to the development and maintenance of a democratic society. It is these freedoms that allow citizens to educate themselves, in an enabling process that enriches both the citizen and the society. Perhaps the most important role libraries will continue to play on the stage of the evolving information society is that of a defender and champion of these basic freedoms for every individual and collectivity.

Further Reading

Betty, Adrienne. *Teacher-Librarians - Leaders who do Make Things Happen.* School Libraries in Canada, 11(1) Fall 1990, pp. 15-18

Bibliotheques scolaires. Numero special. ARGUS 17(4), 1988.

Hall, Noelene. *Teachers, Information and School Libraries.* Paris : UNESCO, General Information Programme and UNISIST, 1986. 100 p. (Report prepared for the IFLA section on School Libraries Working Group PGI-86/WS/17).

Makinta, Y. *The School Library in Nigeria : the need to develop reading culture.* New Library World 94 (1109), 1993. pp. 20-25.

Ojoade, A.B. *Effective Secondary School Libaries for Qualitative Education in Nigeria.* Inspel. 27 (4) 1993. pp. 264-278.

Singh, Diljit. The State of the World's School Libraries. 1994. 21 p. (prepared for the International Association of School Librarianship 23rd Annual Conference, 17-24 July 1994).

Staiger, Ralph C. *Developing the Reading Habit in Children.*

UNESCO, Literacy Lessons, 1990. pp 11-16.

Umunnakwe, U.S. *The Role of School Libraries in Nigerian Education Policy*, Library Review Journal 41 (4), 1992, pp. 49-54.

Ms Marianne Scott
National Librarian
National Library of Canada
395 Wellington Street
Ottawa (Ontario), Canada K1A 0N4

(Source: International Commission on Education for the Twenty First Century)

32

The Role of Libraries and Culture

— *Marianne Scott*

Introduction

The art of writing was created some five thousand years ago by the Sumerians in the Middle East. The means to record information was found to have many uses : religious rites, sacred rituals, official laws, trade agreements, commercial contracts, and treaties between social group could be registered; stories, songs, legends and historical traditions could be preserved and thus contribute to continuity and stability.

If civilization, society and culture depend on the written word to establish fundamental codes and values, the safeguarding of writing depends on libraries. "The urge to keep records and documents corresponds to a deep human instinct. It is therefore not surprising to find evidence in the remains of the earliest known civilizations of the existence of well-developed document - or book repositories." (Frank, 1967). A temple library in the city of Nippur has been dated to the third millennium B.C. ; according to ancient records, the Chinese were keeping archives as early as 2650 B.C. It is thanks to libraries in Athens, Rome and Alexandria that the works of Greek and Roman authors were preserved, while the libraries of Constantinople saved not only Greek texts but Arabic and Byzantine works as well. In western Europe, the Church's libraries were primarily responsible for ensuring the survival of the thought of the ancient world, and provided the necessary resources for adding to knowledge and creative endeavour. The founding of European universities in the eleventh century necessitated the establishment of libraries to permit the development of scholarship.

Historically, libraries have been connected to institutions of government, religion and education. Rameses II of Egypt (r. 1304-1237 B.C.) is said to have established a library of sacred literature in Thebes and placed over the door the inscription "Medicine for the soul" (Krzys, 1968). Many rulers of the ancient Middle East and the Roman Empire established or enriched libraries. In the later Middle Ages the princes of western Europe offered their patronage to the written word and its advocates, while Martin Luther urged the value of public libraries in Germany. It is certain, if not often recognized, that no modern society can function without libraries, and they are essential to developing nations, as has been recognized by UNESCO, which has a tradition of establishing pilot library projects.

It has become common to refer to the late twentieth century as the "Information Age", an accurate description in that there is now more information available in more forms in more parts of the world than at any previous time in history. However, it is equally true that it is becoming more difficult to gather and organize this information, and to ensure that it will be preserved. Perhaps the greatest challenge is the need to select, assess, analyze and intelligently use the information that is available. And while the technology used to gain access to information continues to develop at astonishing speed, the means to deal with social issues such as privacy, economic benefit (or detriment) and control are not being developed at anything like the same rate.

Because information is increasingly valued, it is clear that, more than ever, those individuals and nations that succeed in achieving their goals will be those who know.

Historically, in traditional societies, "memory is regarded as the pre-eminent form of knowledge" (Eliade, 1975). To remember, and to use memory to develop knowledge, it is necessary to have access to the information that will promote memory and permit the formation of knowledge. And those who seek information must know how to use it effectively so as to achieve personal and national goals.

As storehouses of organized, accessible memory and knowledge, libraries are essential to the education of individuals and the development of nations. They can help to reduce or eliminate educational barriers erected by geographic, economic and other factors. However, there are two serious issues that will affect the future use and effectiveness of libraries in all countries, and, consequently, cultural, social and economic development. Many libraries are already providing service to their full capacity, and are increasingly strained by the financial restrictions and resource limitations that have prevailed in recent years. The growing demands on libraries indicate that their value is being recognized by those who use them, but not by those who fund them.

The other issue concerns the perceived worth of reading. Schools are being expected to educate students in ever-diversifying and specialized fields of knowledge, while labouring under the same restrictions that have adversely affected libraries (and other social service institutions). At the same time, it seems inevitable that reading will suffer from the competition offered by the numerous other forms of recreation now available — if, indeed, it is not doing so already. If reading is not inculcated as a habit among young people, it is less likely to become a habit when they are adults.

Simply put, the interest of all societies everywhere warrant a careful re-evaluation of libraries as essential means of storing, organizing and transmitting the cultural products that are vital to education; a re-assessment of the resources assigned to them; and a recognition of the importance that should be placed upon them. There is no simple way to carry out his process; nor will it be inexpensive.

However, if the process is not carried out, it seems probable that the costs, economic, social and cultural, will be far higher. The burning of all books that did not meet with the approval of the First Emperor of China, the destruction of the great library of Alexandria, the dissolution of the monasteries and their accumulated knowledge in England — these and similar disasters are counted among the incalculable impoverishments of culture in human history. The loss of a library means a loss of memory and knowledge. Without memory, there is neither context nor perspective — there is not even a base for building, or rebuilding, the knowledge that might be discovered, or rediscovered. Without libraries there can be no education; without education there can be no progress; without progress there can be no hope. Those who do not know who they have been and who they are now cannot know who they can become.

In the past, a nation's most powerful citizens— princes and priests — where among those who possessed libraries, some of which were opened to scholars in recognition of a library's importance in the growth and spread of knowledge and, consequently, all forms of enrichment. In the future, it will be essential for all citizens to assume the responsibilities, and privileges, of scholars and learn throughout their lives. And it will be the responsibility of governments, and the privilege of those who control and seven in them, to ensure that libraries have the resources necessary to enable citizens to do so.

Further Reading

Francis, Sir Frank (Chalton). "Library", *Chamber's Encyclopedia,* vol. III, Oxford, Pergamon Press, 1967.

Krzys, Richard. "Library Historiography", *Encyclopedia of Library and Information Science*, vol. 15, New York, Marcel

Dekker, 1968, P. 308.

Eliade, Mircea, *Myth and Reality*, trans. W.R. Trask, New York, Harper Colophone Books, 1975, p. 90.

Ms Marianne Scott
National Librarian
National Library of Canada
395 Wellington Street
Ottawa (Ontario) Canada K1A ON4

(Source: International Commission on Education for the Twenty First Century)

33

The Educational Role of Academic Libraries : A Role for the Twenty-First Century

— *Kathleen Delong*

Introduction

Academic libraries contribute to the learning environment and the large educational role of their parent institution by providing library or bibliographic instruction to users. Bibliographic instruction is intended to address the needs of users in the library, educating them in the use of collections and services and introducing them to the new technologies that have accelerated the growth and distribution of information and transformed library systems and processes. Most recently, the term "information literacy" has been coined and used to describe a set of information skills that are an essential element in acquiring an academic degree and in preparing for independent and lifelong learning.

Canadian academic libraries have long recognized the need to instruct their users in the skills required to make good use of library collections and services. In 1988, Beristain surveyed Canadian academic libraries and found instructional programmes firmly entrenched with sound, internationally recognized practices followed and a variety of instructional methods employed.

Instructional programmes are integral to the larger reference or information services associated with academic libraries because they allow library concepts and skills to be taught in an organized and uniform manner to classes or groups of library users. Instruction can be offered on a drop-in or a course-integrated basis, for credit or non-credit. It may be subject-specific or general in nature and it is traditionally concerned with print bibliographic tools, research strategies and methods of citation.

The introduction of new information technologies, such as online catalogues and external databases, has meant that attention must be paid to emerging as well as traditional user information needs and calls into question the sufficiency of traditional bibliographic instruction programmes. A major criticism levelled against bibliographic instruction programmes by Miller (1992) and others is their inherent superficiality. Miller points out that most instructional programmes rely upon passive receipt of information rather than active involvement in the learning process and therefore foster user dependency. He argues that academic librarians have a clear responsibility to teach information skills that will empower library users to become independent learners and researchers. The term "information literacy" has been used by the American Library Association (1989, 22) to describe a skills set that would allow library users to "find, evaluate and use information effectively to solve a particular problem or make a decision."

Incorporating information literacy principles into instructional programmes prepares library users to sort through the myriad of information sources available to them, to evaluate and use the information effectively, in other words, to learn to turn information into knowledge.

Moving from bibliographic instruction to information literacy means a commitment to new teaching and learning styles: resource-centered teaching and active learning. Hancock (1993) stipulates that this shift is essential if we are preparing learners to live and work in the Information

Age. Learners who know how to learn are well-equipped to be lifelong learners and critical consumers of information.

Are Canadian academic libraries prepared to meet the challenge of developing and implementing information literacy programmes? While there is no survey data that would provide an answer to this question, it is important to note that this topic has been taken up in conference programmes at both the national and provincial levels over the last few years. Perhaps of more significance, the strategic plans of two Canadian academic libraries, Dalhousie University and the University of Alberta, define information and research skills as essential to the academic process and specify information literacy as a major strategic initiative for the Library.

Conclusion

Canadian academic libraries play a vital educational role within their respective institutions. There is evident that a shift from bibliographic instruction to information literacy programmes is taking place. This move will ensure that Canada's community of learners and teachers is information-literate, educated to be lifelong learners and well-placed as they move into the twenty first century.

Further Reading

American Library Association. Presidential Committee on Information Literacy. *Final Report,* Chicago, Illinois, American Library Association, 1989 (ERIC Document Reproduction Service No. ED 315 074).

Beristain, Maureen F. Bibliographic Instruction methods and Aids Currently Used in Canadian Academic Libraries. In Elizabeth Frick (Ed.) *A Place to Stand : User Education in Canadian Libraries.* (pp. 41-77). Ottawa, Ontario, Canadian Library Association, 1988.

Breivik, Patricia Senn., and Gee, E. Gordon. *Information Literacy : Revolution in the Library.* New York, ACE/

macmillan 1989.

Hancock, Vivki E. *Information Literacy for Lifelong Learning.* Syracuse, New York, ERIC Clearinghouse on Information Resources, 1993. (ERIC document Reproduction Service No. 358 870.)

Miller, William. The Future of Bibliographic Instruction and Information Literacy for the Academic Librarian. In Betsy Bake & Mary Ellen Litzinger (Eds.) *The Evolving Educational Mission of the Library.* (pp. 140-157). Chicago, Illinois, Association of College and Research Libraries, 1992.

Ms Kathleen DeLong, *Director-at-Large,*
Canadian Association of College and University Libraries, Canadian Library Association
Herbert T. Coutts Library
University of Alberta
Edmonton (Alberta), Canada T6G 2G5

(Source: International Commission on Education for the Twenty First Century)

34

The Role of Large Urban Libraries in the Education Process

— *Josephine Bryant*

The Council of Administrators of Large Urban Public Libraries represents 39 large urban public libraries across Canada serving populations of over 100,000; this is nearly 13 million urban residents, almost half of the population of Canada. In our view of our significant roles is to complement and enhance the formal education system.

Libraries facilitate learning for all ages beginning with the very young and continuing through life. During earlier childhood our print and non-print resources stimulate curiosity and delight children. Students in formal education programmes visit our libraries to complete assignments and to learn new skills. In fact, the historical and contemporary collections and wide-ranging services of large urban public libraries are designed to further support lifelong educational needs.

While funded by the local government and strongly community oriented, the demands of today's users require access to global information. Access to international on-line databases in an established feature of large public libraries, with the consequent necessity of sharing resources through co-operative inter-library lending arrangements. The range of resources is critical because our users live in a multicultural society and have sophisticated reading requirements. We provide multilingual collections and provide accommodation and resources for literacy and second language training classes in association with local education systems.

Through the use of our library collections, we support the individual who must adapt to changing economic and societal circumstances. Our support, therefore, of lifelong learning is very pragmatic, often translating into employment opportunities. Library staff select and organize resources to facilitate access to information and promote their use.

We play a key role in providing opportunities for intellectual growth, stimulation of the imagination, the development of compassionate thought and the cultivation of human feeling so that the individual can arrive at some realization of order and sense of belonging in a changing world.

Public libraries enhance existing educational resources through our longstanding tradition of school and public library co-operation. In addition, we are committed to our important role as part of a learning experience and which furthers the education of adults, whether informally or through the schooling process. By shaping information handling skills, libraries address the individual's lifelong need for knowledge access and assistance. Canadian public libraries are committed to the individual's freedom to choose to read and inquire.

Further Reading

Public Attitudes towards Education in Ontario: the OISE Report. Tornoto, Ontario : Ontario Institute of Studies in Education, 1991.

One Place to Look : the Ontario Public Library Strategic Plan. Toronto, Ontario : Ontario Ministry of Cultural and Communications, Ontario Library Association, 1990.

D'Elia, George and Rodger, Eleanor Jo. "Public Opinion about the Roles of the Public Library in the Community; the results of a recent Gallup poll." *Public Libraries*. January/ February 1994 : p 23-28.

Education and Training in Canada. Ottawa, Ontario : Canada Communication Group. 1992.

Ms Josephine Bryant,
Chair.,Council of Administrators of Large Urban Public Libraries,
North York Public Library
5120 Yonge Street
North York, Ontario - Canada M2N5N9

(Source: International Commission on Education for the Twenty First Century)

35

Canadian Association of Research Libraries

— David McCallum

Introduction

CARL was established in 1976 and consists of 27 university libraries plus the National Library of Canada, and the Canada Institute for Scientific and Technical Information. Membership is institutional, and is open primarily to libraries of Canadian universities which have doctoral graduates in both the arts and sciences. The mission is to increase the capacity of individual member libraries to provide effective support and encouragement to advanced study and research at the national, regional and local levels. In collaboration with the academic community, this mission will be achieved through the pursuit of long-term programmes in the following areas: information policy; resource sharing and scholarly communication.

Research libraries, through their collections and services, have long been central to the pursuit of pure and applied knowledge in universities around the world. Today they are key partners in the educational process itself, promoting information and computer literacy, supporting distance and continuing education programmes and developing new multimedia services based on advanced informatics technologies. Unfortunately, the ability of these libraries to provide access to the world's store of information in all formats is being severely challenged by two significant developments: the worldwide proliferation and runaway prices of scholarly publications; and the complex problem of copyright compliance.

Scholarly Communication: As major purchasers of academic publications, and as providers of services to facilitate access to information in support of research, university libraries are key players in the cycle of scholarly communication. Recently however the proliferation and increasing price of such information (published largely by oligopolies outside of North America), coupled with a global economic situation that is unlikely to improve in the near future, has required university libraries to cut back on acquisitions to such an extent that the comprehensiveness of their collections cannot help but deteriorate. And while advances in electronic networking technology hold out the promise of providing an alternative vehicle for the distribution of scholarly information, many issues remain to be addressed before such an avenue becomes viable.

The Association is currently developing a proposal aimed at informing the Canadian university community of key issues facing research libraries, particularly the economic dimensions of the scholarly communication crisis, with the ultimate objective being agreement on appropriate cooperative action. The need to change prevailing attitudes on the part of the professorate with respect to current publishing models will be given particular attention.

Copyright : The question of copyright cannot help but be of prime concern to research libraries. Copying for convenience (as opposed to copying to avoid purchase) is a common occurrence in CARL member institutions, and is central to the operation of the interlibrary loan system. While the Association supports fair compensation for creators, it strongly believes that certain types of copying should not trigger compensatory payments to copyright holders and has vigorously put its case forward to consultative groups established by the Canadian government over the years.

Much to the chagrin of the Canadian library community, the federal government of the day decided to introduce only certain aspects of revised copyright legislation (Phase I) in 1988, though swift introduction of the second wave of amendments (Phase II) was promised. The phase, which is expected to include such vital aspects as exceptions for library and educational uses of copyright material, has been eagerly awaited ever since.

Despite the fact that electronic networking technology is increasingly used for library and distance education applications, Phase II will not address such uses. Since it is virtually inevitable that yet another legislative round will be necessary to provide legal guidelines in this regard, it is vital that Phase II is swiftly and successfully concluded, and that research begins as soon as possible into copyright in the context of electronic information exchange.

Conclusion

In the area of scholarly communication, the formation of a small committee consisting of several Canadian Academic Vice-Presidents and members of CARL will be a first step in the process described above. The establishment of this group will open a useful communications channel to key university decision-makers that should capitalize on the growing awareness of library and related information problems on the part of senior university administrators and provide a forum for discussion of realistic ways to address them. In the area of copyright, two efforts are being proposed : i) a concerted lobbying effort for swift introduction and passage of Phase II legislation; and ii) researching the interface between electronic networking and intellectual property in preparation for future Canadian legislative initiatives. The Association hopes that it will be possible to co-operative on these issues with foreign and international bodies who are no doubt developing their own initiatives to address similar concerns.

Mr. David McCallum
Executive Director
Canadian Association of Research Libraries
Room 602 - Morisset Hall
University of Ottawa
65 University Street
Ottawa (Ontario) Canada K1N 9A5

(Source: International Commission on Education for the Twenty First Century)

36

The International Federation of Workers' Educational Associations

— *Aaron Barnea*

Every participatory democratic political theorist from Socrates to Rousseau to Jefferson to Dewey has emphasized that democracy is a learned pattern of behaviour that can only be acquired through practice. People learn to behave democratically through exercising the rights and responsibilities of citizenship in democratic institutions; institutions remain democratic because sufficient numbers of people have acquired the basic competencies of self governance required for effective institutional functioning.

In the history of democratic societies, free trade unions have been one of the most important institutions for teaching the basic skills required for democratic citizenship. Trade unions develop democratic competence in several ways : 1) because they are internally structured as democratic institutions they provide their members with opportunities to participate in the governance of the institutions in different capacities : 2) in order to improve their own institutional functioning and remain democratic, they provide their members and leaders with considerable training and education in the various skills required for democratic leadership and participation; 3) they call attention to the need for an economy that is both productive and equitable in order to generate the standard of living required for democratic political systems to flourish; 4) They use their influence and resources consistently to try to democratize the broader education system of the society in order to allow each individual the opportunity to develop his/her knowledge, skill and potential to the fullest.

The International Workers' Education Movement has its roots in these basic trade union values and policies. Workers Education, as a field of practice, has historically been dedicated to make life-long learning and development available to everyone who wishes it. Workers' Education is organized around the concept that democratizing education is integral to democratizing society. This means not only democratizing *access* to education but also *democratizing the learning process itself* so that the learners have influence over the content and methodology of what they learn. There is now a well-developed body of research evidence that suggests that democratizing the learning process is not only good politics but is also good pedagogy. In countless studies, it has become clear that learner influence on the learning process is a major predictor of success on a wide variety of learning outcome measures from test scores to performance to interest in the subject matter (these results are not confined to adults but apply equally well to children).

Workers's Education has also been organized around the concept of cooperation learning - the idea that for many learning tasks people learn better working together with others. Adult worker educators pioneered many of the techniques of cooperative learning now making their way in the formal primary, secondary and even higher education systems.

A third organizing characteristic of Workers' Education methodology is the appropriate use of the non-formal learning context and strategy. Formal learning opportunities are often unavailable or unfeasible for many adult workers in many contexts. Workers educators have been leaders in developing non-formal learning-teaching strategies aimed at conveying important knowledge in accessible formats outside the formal learning systems. Worker educators have also been leaders in calling attention to the important role of work activity itself in stimulating or constraining worker interest in access to opportunities for further learning and qualification development. The Workers' Education Movement has been an active voice for the transformation of work organization and work activity to create meaningful work roles that demand and allow continuous learning, growth and development for all workers.

Workers' Education also has an emphasis on developing tolerance and appreciation of diversity. Because trade union institutions are typically heterogeneous, worker educators have been leaders in developing educational strategies for teaching individuals from different racial, ethnic, religious, class and gender groups the tolerance required for democracy to flourish in pluralist societies and institutions. Such educational approaches are critical as international trade becomes increasingly important and previously homogeneous societies become more heterogeneous.

All of these characteristics and others of Workers' Education mean that the Workers' Education Movement plays an important role in the linking of "Education, citizenship and democracy". This role will be more important in the creation of an international strategy designated to help democracy grow and flourish in the Twenty-first Century as the world adjusts to new economic and political realities.

Mr Aaron Barnea
Secretary-General
International Federation of Workers' Education Associations (IFWEA)
c/o Histadrut, 93 Arlozorov St.
62098 Tel-Aviv, Israel

(Source: International Commission on Education on the Twenty First Century)

37

The United World Colleges

— David Sutcliffe

The United World Colleges have been active in the field of international higher secondary education since 1962, when the first College, the Atlantic College, was founded in South Wales in the United Kingdom. In just over thirty years, the United World Colleges (UWC) movement has founded a total of eight colleges, sited in Wales, Singapore, Canada, Swaziland, the USA, Italy, Venezuela and Hong King. New Colleges will open in Norway (1995) and India (1997-98).

The Original Concept

Young men and women between the ages of 16 and 19 are at a specially impressionable and formative age. Attitudes of mind can be cast at this stage as at no other. Idealism and curiosity about the world, a readiness to embrace and absorb new experiences and to adapt a new cultures and ways of thinking, are combined and shaped by an awareness of one's own roots and traditions. This is the time when the critical decisions are being prepared about one's future career and life's work, yet the pressure of university studies and professional training are not yet dominant. The UWC offer scholarships for an international experience of two years to young people from all over the world, chosen on personal merit, irrespective of family, financial, political, religious or social background.

The key element is the formation of international

attitudes within a programme which combines rigorous academic work for university entry with an equally challenging involvement in community and environmental service. The course lasts two years. The academic programme leads to the Diploma of the International Baccalaureate.

The First Colleges

These are two-year, all scholarship and fully residential colleges which do not have private, fee paying entry. Competition for the places is very severe - there are often 20 and more applicants for each place.

The scholarship entry ensures students of unusual quality and commitment. Scholarship programmes funded, for example, by the Canadian Development Agency (CIDA) and the Italian Foreign Office, have enabled many outstanding students from the developing world and the countries of Central and Eastern Europe to take part.

More Recent Developments

UWC has not wished to be confined to a single model. The UWC of South East Asia in Singapore is an international comprehensive school of some 1300 pupils of ages 12 to 18. The senior pupils study for the International Baccalaureate, undertake community service, and have a particularly impressive range of projects for the direct assistance of Third World countries in their area. The UWC of Southern Africa, in Swazailand, also an "all age school", has, naturally enough, a special commitment to combat racism and apartheid. It was founded in 1963 in protest against South African policies, and as an example of what might be achieved if young people from all races were brought up together. It is certainly no accident that Nelson Mandela, Archbishop Tutu and many other prominent members of the anti-apartheid movement, have sent their children to the college. The Simon Boliver College in Venezuela is a new departure. It was conceived after discussions between the then International President of UWC, HRH the Prince of

Wales and the President of Venezuela. It provides a three-year course in practical agricultural management, with an emphasis on sound environmental practice, and a determination to bridge the characteristic gap in Third World countries between the agricultural scientist and the worker on the land.

Short courses also aim to offer participants a concentrated three-week exposure to the ideals of the United World Colleges. These take place regularly in the Andes and intermittently in Malta, Israel, Cyprus and Lilthuania.

The Potential Wider Significance of the United World Colleges

The colleges have always wished to share their unique experience with others, and it will be clear that, in the ex-student organization or Network there is to hand a substantial group of very able men and women with a strongly formative experience behind them. Ways in which the UWC experience might be exploited by like-minded organizations include the following : a) **Upper Secondary Education :** The Colleges have historically exerted a powerful influence on the International Baccalaureate, above all in its early days. Now, the colleges are seeking to introduce to their own students new programmes on Global and Environmental concerns and Conflict Resolution as an integral part of the pre-university diploma. Success in these ventures could well stimulate innovation in other systems, of education as well as the International Baccalaureate; b) **Cultural Communication :** UWC students enter the scholarship colleges at the age of 16 or 17 from their own national systems, not from the international community. The ways in which the colleges promote inter-culture communication within their communities and the study of international affairs might repay documentation and study for their possible application in other contexts. Notable throughout the generations and across all colleges has been the lesson that a two-year international experience of the kind, during which the students must articulate their own cultures and national habits to often skeptical and critical contemporaries, leads to a deeper and richer comprehension of their own background, combined with a far greater readiness to accept the real richness of diversity; c) **Community Service :** All UWC students spend a number of hours each week working with the disabled and marginalised in their local society. There is potential for a vast extension of the contacts and knowledge already available and which could be extended to other schools and their pupils throughout the world; d) **Teacher Education :** Over thirty years, the UWC have obviously employed a significant number of teachers of many different nationalities, many of whom have returned to serve their own national state schools. It may fairly be claimed that the teacher training potential of the colleges has yet scarcely been recognized, let along exploited and made available to others.

Conclusion

The UWC, founded as a private initiative at the height of the Cold War, have grown into an organization which benefits from substantial governmental as well as private and foundation funding. The thirty years have seen steady expansion, and the movement is now poised for new initiatives involving other existing international schools, vocational education, projects more sensitive to the needs of developing countries, new short courses, and cooperation with a large variety of like-minded international bodies.

David Sutcliffe
Head
United World College of the Adriatic
Via Trieste 29
34013 Duino (Trieste) Italy

(Source: International Commission on Education for the Twenty First Century)

38

The International Association for Students Interested in Economics and Management (AIESEC International)

— *Diego Molano*

AIESEC (Association Internationale des etudiants en sciences economiques et commerciales), the largest organization of its kind in the world, has promoted international co-operation and understanding of other cultures since 1948. By providing the student community with international exposure, management skills and an insight into the issues of today, AIESEC ensures that these individuals will take on a leading role in society, both now and in the future, AIESEC is a positive force in global development.

The world is experiencing unprecedented and irreversible changes. The development leads increasingly towards globalisation, interdependence, complexity and increasing uncertainties for the future.

Despite the amazing advances in science and technology as well as visible signs of social and economical progress, humankind is at a stage of unparalleled inequalities among the people of the world.

Never has the gap between rich and poor, between educated and illiterate, between nourished and the hungry been so dramatic. The economic, social and environmental challenges make international co-operation and global citizenship an imperative.

In order to develop the society of the future based on the realities of the current world situation, we should first ask ourselves: What kind of society do we want for the future and which are the characteristics every individual should have to enable him or her to live in global society? We should question education and how it can lead the process to achieve this ideal society. It is impossible to continue discussing about education without knowing which education for what kind of society. Otherwise we will go back to the same stage where the future is not taken into consideration for the future direction in the educational process. Education should take a proactive role building up the society of the next century. The society of the 21st century should have the following major characteristics :

- co-operation between nations and individuals to ensure development;
- inter-cultural interaction without any tension
- respect and tolerance for others
- high sense of responsibility amongst individuals, groups and society for the future of the world (Commission III output, AIESEC International Congress 1993)

These should be core values and a basis for individual, group and social behaviour. They can be developed through formal and informal education. The inter-relation, the balance and the effectiveness of both educational processes should be analyzed in order to maximize all the possibilities to develop every individual.

The development of this kind of education should start from the analysis of the current educational system and structures, taking into consideration the following areas: 1) **Content of Education** - Not only related to knowledge and techniques, but also to values and aptitude that every individual has to acquire. It is not enough to have access to basic knowledge but also to advance knowledge for all sectors in society, which enables each individual to have an opportunity for long life learning and improvement of quality of life; 2) **Structure of Educational Systems** - The current structures are not equipped to accept the inter-relation and interaction of formal and informal education. There are certain areas like pre-natal education and third age education that should be considered as a part of the whole educational process of every individual; 3) **Educational Methodologies** - More interactive processes should be developed between teachers and students. Additionally it is important at all levels of education from primary education to higher education to get an interaction between old and new generations and also with other sectors in society, such as government, private sector or independent organization. Finally, more practical experience and international exposure for students should be promoted.

There are certain global issues or world problems that should become the major topics to be addressed in the future through formal and informal education: a) international co-operation for development ; b) promotion of human rights but at the same time human responsibilities; c) peace and understanding among nations and cultures; d) drugs and violence; e) values and ethics; f) participation in society. Finding their causes and analysis of their solutions should be a fundamental part of any educational process. The promotion and build up of these sets of values to overcome scme of these issues in the future should be a priority.

Involvement of Student Association : The main strengths of student organizations are direct contact with students, and for many years our associations have been working in the educational field. Having similar objectives to the commission, we feel it is our responsibility to contribute to this process with our network and experience. We have identified the following areas in which we are or could be actively involved with the objectives of the commission : a) **Gathering and Distribution of Information** - Student associations could play an important role in collecting and making information about education accessible to all students and interested sectors in their respective areas. Surveys and research can be organized in order to determine different priorities and activities of education; b) **Providing Feedback and Playing an Active Role in Preparation for New Proposals** - all sectors have been invited to participate in the process of improving the current situation. Educational institutions, the corporate sector, NGOs, and last but by no means least, students, are to be heard and involved in policy making. It is only through this co-operation that we can build a hopeful future for education in terms of equity and efficiency; c) **Co-operation with Teaching Research** - seminars and conferences on various topics are being organized by students organizations. These activities aim at complementing education in different fields. In 1990 AIESEC fully implemented the Global theme Programme. The present theme is *"Education towards International and Cultural Understanding"*, whose primary objective is to look for new and practical ways to educate people for a society with international and cultural understanding; d) **Partnership with Economic Life** - The university and educational institutions cannot be isolated and outside of the normal education, training activities and practical experience should be provided Student associations should cooperate with the working world and facilitate these processes; e) improvement of communication, international mind, languages skills - international student association can provide the management, communication and language skills for future development in countries. The possibility of joining such an organization gives students the chance to develop new initiative in an international context. The potential of student network to play an important role in future educational programmes can be fully accomplished only by the decisive support on behalf of the educational authorities at all levels.

The problems related to education differ greatly from country to country. However, the various educational processes - formal and informal - have to assume their role in the creation of a new global society. The issues being addressed and the solutions to promote should be developed with the participation of different sectors in society, especially based on the expectation of young people of the future, because they should live in the society of the twenty-first century and also they should participate actively in building it up.

Diego Molano
Vice President of Programmes
AIESEC International
40 rue Washington
B-1050 Brussels - Belgium

(Source: International Commission on Education for the Twenty First Century)

39

New Ways of Thinking About Learning and the World of Work : A Canadian Perspective

— *Ian Morrison*

Introduction

Capital, technology, raw materials and information flow freely across borders. The only component of production that is unique to each nation is its work force.

Those countries that have well-trained, flexible workers and modern infrastructure attract global investment in an upward spiral consistent with the ever increasing skills and experience of the work force.

This increases worker compensation and raises the standard of living.

Level and distribution of educational attainment affect competitive position and the capacity to adjust.

Recent times have given rise to "good jobs" which are well paying, long-term and knowledge-based, and "bad jobs" which are unstable, short-term, part-time and low paying.

Invention and mass-production require a highly skilled, flexible work force.

The individual must be able to flow with ease into

and out of work, learning and leisure involvements.

It is necessary to act on, not just talk about, a movement from front-end education to a model of learning throughout life.

New definitions of what constitutes productive involvement in the economy and society are required.

New and flexible forms of work organization and hours of work are needed.

People with the most education have the highest earnings.

Employers are most likely to sponsor the continuing education of male managers.

Substantial remedial action is required to ensure job opportunities for young people.

Barriers to adult learner participation need to be minimized and access enhanced.

Employees need the basic numeracy and literacy skills on which to build.

Citizens should have access to learning opportunities throughout life.

Citizens should have access to funding and necessary services to support their learning throughout life.

Employers need to take greater responsibility for the continuous learning of all employees. This should decrease wage bidding for high demand skills and increase employee loyalty, motivation and competence.

Employers should provide paid educational leave.

Government should work with other stakeholders to ensure learner access to educational opportunities and work throughout life.

Learning should be a means, not an end. Learning

strengthens citizenship and the contribution which individuals can make to a strong civil society.

Inequities in access to learning opportunities and hobs between sexes, between generations, and between groups in society must be overcome.

Special efforts will be required to ensure that learning disadvantaged people, and the cohort of young people following the very large "baby boom" generation, have access to new and emerging job opportunities.

Mr. Ian Morrison
Executive Director
Canadian Association for Adult Education
Corbett House
29 Prince Arthur Avenue
Toronto (Ontario) M5R 1B2, Canada

(Source: International Commission on Education for the Twenty First Century)

40

Draft Plan for Educational Reform in Korea

—*Woo-Tak Chung*

The world today is overflowing with enthusiasm for educational reform. The question of educational reform has become a topic of national concern. It is natural that Korea should endeavour to reform its system of education. The Presidential Commission on Education Reform (PCER) was established by the Presidential decree of President Kim Young Sam in 1994. Educational reform in Korea must solve two major problems : first, to cure educational diseases like ▪ crammer education, ▪ exam hells, and ▪ excessive out-of-school lessons. Second, to suggest new education for future generations to lead successful lives in the 21st century. As preparation for the society of the 21st century characterized by humanization, globalization, and high-tech and information, the PCER states its basic aims for educational reform in accordance with the following four main objectives: ▪education for dignified human life, ▪educational diversification, ▪ high-quality education, ▪cultivation of new human resources. For this purpose, the PCER is examining the following matters : ▪basic educational policies and educational reform, ▪plans for the short-and long term development of education; ▪the inspection and evaluation of the status quo of educational reform currently underway.

Draft Plan for Education Reform

The Presidential Commission on Education Reform

(PCER) of the Republic of Korea drafted its comprehensive plan as follows :

Three Strategies for Immediate Implementation

■ **Expanding Educational Financing :** Financing is the key factor in determining the quality of education, educational conditions and commitment to educational reforms. The PCER proposed to increase educational financing as follows:

1. Priority adjustment in the national education budget : ● to increase the rate of grants for local education, ● to create a special account for improvement of educational facilities and environment.
2. Additional taxation for education: ● to impose and increase education taxes from various sources including land taxes, town planning taxes and inhabitant taxes.
3. Mobilizing the private sector : ● to allow donations from parents, ● to encourage contributions from private companies.

■ **Strengthening the Competitiveness of Universities :** The quantitative expansion of higher education in Korea has produced many incompetent universities. To enhance the academic standard of universities and to strengthen the competitiveness of them, the PCER recommended the following policies :

1. Diversification and specialization of the university model : (a) to abolish government's direct regulations on academic affairs, (b) to encourage autonomous university reform.
2. Innovation of education and research systems : (a) to strengthen the quality and credibility of doctoral courses, (b) to provide government subsidies based on the evaluation of faculty members' research activities, (c) to strengthen the government's financial support for the strengthening of university libraries and laboratories to

the standard of the advanced countries.

3. Autonomy of the higher education administration : (a) to improve the quality of university management and administration, (b) to develop a new legal status of the national universities for their effective and efficient management, (c) to revise accounting and auditing systems for the autonomous administration, (d) disseminate the results of the university evaluations to the public.

■ **Expanding the Autonomy and Responsibility of Private School :** Because educational administration in Korea has been highly centralized, private schools are now under strict control by the central and local government. In 1993, the percentage of private schools was 25.6% in middle schools, 61.9% in high schools, 95.3% in junior colleges, and 75.6% in universities. The PCER recommended to the President to allow private schools to select their students and decide their tuition fees autonomously: 1) Selective support for the private primary and middle schools : (a) to allow free competition for the entrance to private high schools, (b) to permit private schools to determine tuition fees autonomously, (c) to emphasize specialization in private schools, (d) to provide financial support based on results of evaluation and accreditation of universities.

Eight Strategies for Medium-term Reform

1. Reform of the entrance examination system for universities : (a) to select students throughout the year, (b) to guarantee multiple-applications for admission to universities, (c) to innovate the achievement record system of high schools from a comparative to an absolute system of evaluation.

2. Diversification and flexibility of the school system, (a) to integrate kindergarten into the public education system, (b) to diversify the present 6-3-3-4 pattern of the school system.

3. Curriculum reform in the primary and middle school: (a) to reduce the number of required subjects and encourage discussion, practical training, experimentation and voluntary service, (b) to strengthen moral, cultural and art education, (c) to revise the textbook compilation system, (d) to reinforce foreign language education and education for international understanding, (e) to provide a relevant education for scientifically gifted students.

4. Enhancement of teacher quality and improvement of teacher status: (a) to upgrade the status of teachers through various incentives, (b) to enlarge the opportunities for in-service teacher training, (c) to adjust teacher salaries so as to be competitive with other occupations, and increase fringe benefits, (d) to enhance teacher professionalism.

5. Management and administration by the "school community" : (a) to create a "board of school management" at the individual school level, consisting of the school master, teachers, parents and community leaders, (b) to encourage the democratization of the school administration, (c) to grant autonomy in the organization of educational programmes in view of local needs.

6. Innovation of technical and vocational education : (a) to innovate 2 + 1 system of technical high schools in order to facilitate graduates' practical operations, (b) to encourage the specialization of the junior vocational colleges, (c) to develop open universities as a centre for technical and vocational education at the higher education level.

7. Amendments to the education laws : (a) to amend education laws and related ordinances in order to ensure the people's right to education and guarantee educational reforms.

8. Strengthening of lifelong education : (a) to open schools and universities to the local communities to provide life-long education services, (b) to upgrade the quality of the Educational Broadcasting System, (c) to encourage family education.

Further Reading

The Republic of Korea, *The Presidential Commission on Education Reform (Brochure).* Seoul, 1994.

The President Commission for Education Reform. *Korean Education Reform Toward the 21st Century,* Seoul, 1987.

idem. Draft Report on Education Reform. Seoul, 1994.

Woo-Tak Chung
Associate expert
UNESCO (International Commission on Education for the Twenty First Century)
7, Place de Fontenoy
75352 Paris 07 SP - France

(Source: International Commission on Education for the Twenty First Century)

41

Renaissance for the Young Child in the 21st Century : The Challenge and the Opportunity

— UNICEF

Recognizing the advantages of a collaborative process in the early stages of policy development, UNICEF gathered a group of international child development experts to help sharpen our thinking and clarify our principles as we move forward from policy formulation to the articulation of specific actions. Following a review of the principles for action, principles for learning and the typology of complementary programming strategies that undergird UNICEF's current policy, the meeting began with a more focused analysis of three accepted strategies. These included parent education, community partnerships and linkages with programmes for vulnerable children. For each of these strategies an attempt was made to assess: where we have been; why is more focused attention required; what principles for action should guide our work; and finally, what specific interventions should be pursued.

Parent education programmes - those that strengthen parents and caregivers' child development knowledge, skills and practices - have emerged as the cornerstone of UNICEF's ECD (Early Childhood Development) strategies. Utilizing a combination of intervention channels, including the media, the discussion focused on the need to recognize parents as the first and primary educators of their children, and the most important component of long-term enhanced child and family outcomes. It was emphasized that the tremendous variability in how parents rear children must be balanced alongside universal child behaviours and parental responses. A typology of options regarding the participation of parents in various ECD activities was proposed.

The discussion of community partnerships began with an assessment of why participation is critical and what we have learned from the past. A wide range of innovative strategies to incorporate the existing skills and talents of communities as, for example, creating hybrids of insider-outsider expertise was presented. Participants acknowledged that the participation of community members in ECD activities returns benefits directly to the community as well as to families and their children. In addition, other less direct benefits included the consideration of cultural specificities, the provision of services closer to potential users and the increased likelihood of promoting integrated service delivery through community associations.

Capitalizing on knowledge gained through past initiatives, strategies to reach children in areas affected by organized violence, children with disabilities, and the health, education and protection of young girls must be implemented. Regarding our capacity for interventions directed to these more difficult groups, several challenges were highlighted. To what extent can existing ECD materials and methods be directly transferred to these more targeted groups of children—how and in what ways do they need to be adapted? Secondly, it is crucial that the operationalization of linkages be carefully and realistically analyzed. In a system structured by programme content, how can we form bridges across sectors to prevent parallel programme development? Finally, how can we tap into existing materials and expertise and uncover what already exists? At the same time, new crises requiring immediate responses emerge every day. How can we respond more efficiently to these changing circumstances and monitor what was learned in the process.

The Challenge: Cross-cutting Implementation Issues

In addition to the challenges of understanding the cost and financing of ECD and of overcoming the existing inertia surrounding monitoring and evaluation, several recurring implementation issues emerged throughout the discussions. They resurfaced once again as participants described the set of obstacles and barriers hampering the implementation of ECD programmes. Among these were: lack of multi-level training schemes; absence of materials combined with difficulties of distribution and dissemination; pilot-level initiatives which cannot achieve scale; large-scale programmes which cannot be sustained; and rigid infrastructure resistant to innovative methods. Mention was made of the fact that diverse national contexts present quite different opportunities, resources and constraints when implementing ECD programmes, and that generic principles of ECD programming must be adapted to these varied contexts in order to be effective. Programme adaptations are needed in countries facing anarchy and war (such as in former Yugoslavia, Somalia, Liberia and Sierra Leone), extreme poverty (as in South Asia or sub-Saharan Africa), major poverty (for instance in Latin America, Indochina and West Asia), as well as in emerging industrial states (e.g. Thailand, Malaysia, Mexico, Middle East) and mature economies (such as Europe and North America).

The discussion of such concerns, while not new to educational practitioners and programmers, was however accompanied with insight and the hint of optimism which comes from the creative identification of potential solutions. In this regard, a key task was proposed; to replicate, increase coverage and document carefully those agreed upon principles. This would extend the state-of-the-art beyond the collection of interesting policy declarations and smaller-scale activities which have characterized the field to date.

Strategic activities were identified, as indicated below:

- Design an action research agenda, based on updated or recently designed policies, which is developed at national and regional levels to ensure the improvement of policies, plans and programmes for ECD. Sustain documentation efforts which test and disseminate innovations quickly.
- Faster continuous high-level policy dialogue through advocacy interventions, such as regional fora, and formulation of orientations for-governments regarding local initiatives for ECD.
- Forge multisectoral and multilevel linkages to ensure comprehensive, continuous and integrated programming, beginning with prenatal education and health care to preparation for success in primary school. Build alliances with governments NGOs and research bodies, as well as technical and community institutions for the same purpose.
- Develop monitoring and evaluation mechanisms which allow for continual adjustment and refinement of preventive and remedial interventions.
- Explore, develop and utilize the tremendous potential of communication and media technology to enhance all aspects of programme planning, design, implementation and evaluation, within and across countries and regions.
- Promote participatory planning and utilization of results in the design of programme strategies.
- Reorient preschool education programmes towards home-based and community-based programmes with parents' empowerment as a main feature.
- Ensure linkages of innovative pilot activities with larger-scale national efforts.
- Focus on training, and particularly training of trainers.

The Opportunity: Policy Formulation

The discussion peaked with an enthusiastic and emotional plea to the international community to redefine, in broad conceptual terms, the role and function of ECD initiatives within the human development arena. Six recommendations were put forth:

- To include ECD in a broader frame work of human capacity enhancement, and make it an entry point for any human development strategy.
- To pursue the development of inclusionary models of child, family and community development; *inter alia* addressing principles of professionalism and valuing quality.
- To consider ECD as a foundation of basic education, and not only as a major supportive strategy. ECD is more than a need to be met. Rather it is a means to achieve quality learning. In this respect, minimum quality standards should also be developed and be part of any intervention in favour of the young child.
- To ensure that in any overall approach to ECD, current ideas, cultural patterns and practices from all regions of the world be equally represented, respected and understood.
- To continue to promote a holistic approach to young child development, taking into consideration both the health and nutritional aspects of the child, and his or her emotional and social needs.
- To move away from donor-driven development by promoting collaboration between the donor community and the host countries in order to ensure appropriate identification of priorities and to pursue innovative strategies to attract sustainable sources of funds.

If the overall goals of the workshop was to forge new

alliances while solidifying existing linkages, and to bring closure to the successes and the failures of our past while shedding light on the directions of the future, then the group of child development experts assembled in Florence did indeed see the dawn of a renaissance for the young child in the 21st century.

(Source : Early Childhood Development Revisited : From Policy Formulation to Programme Implementation, 1995)

42

Africa : A Fresh Start

— *Fay Chung*

The quest for a blend of African traditions with the universal values that will shape the next century.

More than any other continent, Africa needs to rethink its education systems. All too often, the systems of education inherited from colonialism have been preserved in Africa more or less intact, generally on the grounds of "maintaining standards". What this actually means is that a very small elite enjoys exactly the same kind of education as it would have in Europe, while the vast majority are deprived of any form of modern education whatever.

The failure of these educated elites to transform their countries from feudal social structures and traditional subsistence agriculture is in marked contrast with the success of the East Asian elites who have managed to make their economies more efficient than the Western economies that they began by imitating. Why have African elites failed whereas their counterparts in East Asia have succeeded so spectacularly? What role has education played in this?

The Japanese Model

East Asia has been strongly influenced by the Japanese model. In the nineteenth century, the Japanese realized that it was essential for their survival as a nation to appropriate Western mathematics, science and technology, whilst eschewing Western culture and social values.

Compulsory primary education for all existed in Japan by 1870. The goal of secondary education for all was subsequently achieved, and after the Second World War access to post-secondary education became available for the majority. But while they sought to imitate, and later to surpass, Western science and technology, the Japanese insisted on the primacy of their own language, literature, culture and religion.

Africa has not made such a conscious choice. The introduction of Western education into Africa by Christian missionaries meant that the educated elite was more steeped in Christian theology, history, literature and culture than in science and technology. This strong bias towards the humanities still exists today.

Probably the most visible symptom of this Western orientation was the rejection of African languages in the education system. Even now African languages are not taught in most French-or Portuguese-speaking countries, and even some English-speaking countries have denigrated the use of African languages as 'divisive' and 'tribalistic'. To the African Christian convert African culture was synonymous with superstition and backwardness and was generally rejected as 'uncivilized'. In other words, the educated African adopted the European conception of traditional African culture.

Redefining the Purpose of Education

Very few African countries have attained primary education for all, despite the fact that many have been independent for some thirty years. At the secondary level, the record is even worse. Many African countries only provide secondary education for 4 to 5 per cent of the appropriate age group. In most African countries, less than one percent of the relevant age group goes on to any form of post-secondary education, compared to between 25 and 75 per cent in the industrialized countries. Those who do are unlikely to specialize in science or technology.

It is within this context that we need to re-examine the connection between education and economic development on the one hand, and education and cultural values on the other. "Development" must be defined more clearly. At present Africa's development strategy appears to be based almost exclusively on structural adjustment, although this is clearly a far too narrow and economist conceptualization of development, which does not take into account such extremely important factors as a country's level of human-resource development or its level of economic diversification and industrialization.

Education also needs to be redefined. The systems and structures of the past should not be retained uncritically. Education must serve a purpose, and Africa needs to decide what that purpose is. While it has a critical role to play in economic development, it has an equally important role in creating and defining the values that will make Africa politically and culturally united, coherent and forward-looking. Only when the purpose of education has been clearly defined can Africa decide what type of education is suitable for its development.

In deciding on that purpose the global village and the global market must be kept in mind. It is no longer possible for Africa to perpetuate its colonial and feudal heritages by continuing with the educational systems and structures of the past whilst ignoring the transformation of the rest of the world into technologically advanced industrialized economies. On the other hand, Africa is the least polluted and least environmentally damaged continent. As the latest entrant into the modernization process, it may be able to avoid the terrible environmental and human damage caused by the process.

Fay Chung

Education Cluster, UNICEF, New York

(Source: The UNESCO Courier, April 1996)

43

World Declaration on Education for All

Meeting Basic Learning Needs

PREAMBLE

More than 40 years ago, the nations of the world, speaking through the Universal Declaration of Human Rights, asserted that "everyone has a right to education". Despite notable efforts by countries around the globe to ensure the right to education for all, the following realities persist:

- More than 100 million children, including at least 60 million girls, have no access to primary schooling;
- More than 960 million adults, two-thirds of whom are women, are illiterate, and functional illiteracy is a significant problem in all countries, industrialized and developing;
- More than one third of the world's adults have no access to the printed knowledge, new skills and technologies that could improve the quality of their lives and help them shape, and adapted to social and cultural change; and
- More than 100 million children and countless adults fail to complete basic education programmes; millions more satisfy the attendance requirements but do not acquire essential knowledge and skills;

At the same time, the world faces daunting problems;

notably mounting debt burdens, the threat of economic stagnation and decline, rapid population growth, widening economic disparities among and within nations, war, occupation, civil strife, violent crime, the preventable deaths of millions of children and widespread environmental degradation. These problems constrain efforts to meet basic learning needs, while the lack of basic education among a significant proportion of the population prevents societies from addressing such problems with strength and purpose.

These problems have led to major setbacks in basic education in the 1980s in many of the least developed countries. In some other countries, economic growth has been available to finance education expansion, but even so, many millions remain in poverty and unschooled or illiterate. In certain industrialized countries too, cutbacks in government expenditure over the 1980s have led to the deterioration of education.

Yet the world is also at the threshold of a new century, with all its promise and possibilities. Today, there is genuine progress towards peaceful detente and greater cooperation among nations. Today, the essential rights and capacities of women are being realized. Today, there are many useful scientific and cultural developments. Today, the sheer quantity of information available in the world-much of it relevant to survival and basic well being -is exponentially greater than that available only a few years ago, and the rate of its growth is accelerating. This includes information about obtaining more life enhancing knowledge - or learning how to learn. A synergistic effect occurs when important information is coupled with another modern advance—our new capacity to communicate.

These new forces, when combined with the cumulative experience of reform, innovation, research and the remarkable educational progress of many countries, make the goal of basic education for all—for the first time in history—an attainable goal.

Therefore, we participants in the World Conference on Education for All, assembled in Jomtien, Thailand, from 5 to 9 March, 1990 :

Recalling that education is a fundamental right for all people, women and men, of all ages, throughout our world;

Understanding that education can help ensure a safer, healthier more prosperous and environmentally sound world, while simultaneously contributing to social, economic, and cultural progress, tolerance, and international cooperation;

Knowing that education is an indispensable key to, though not a sufficient condition for, personal and social improvement;

Recognizing that traditional knowledge and indigenous cultural heritage have a value and validity in their own right and a capacity to both define and promote development;

Acknowledging that, overall, the current provision of education is seriously deficient and that it must be made more relevant and qualitatively improved, and made universally available;

Recognizing that sound basic education is fundamental to the strengthening of higher levels of education and of scientific and technological literacy and capacity and thus to self-reliant development; and

Recognizing the necessity to give to present and coming generations an expanded vision of, and a renewed commitment to, basic education to address the scale and complexity of the challenge;

proclaim the following

World Declaration on Education for All: Meeting Basic Learning Needs

EDUCATION FOR ALL : THE PURPOSE

ARTICLE 1 ● MEETING BASIC LEARNING NEEDS

1. Every person—child, youth and adult—shall be able to benefit from educational opportunities designed to meet their basic learning needs. These needs comprise both essential learning tools (such as literacy, oral expression, numeracy, and problem solving) and the basic learning content (such as knowledge, skills, values, and attitudes) required by human beings to be able to survive, to develop their full capacities, to live and work in dignity, to participate fully in development, to improve the quality of their lives, to make informed decisions, and to continue learning. The scope of basic learning needs and how they should be met varies with individual countries and cultures, and inevitably, changes with the passage of time.

2. The satisfaction of these needs empowers individuals in any society and confers upon them a responsibility to respect and build upon their collective cultural, linguistic and spiritual heritage, to promote the education of others, to further the cause of social justice, to achieve environmental protection, to be tolerant towards social, political and religious systems which differ from their own, ensuring that commonly accepted humanistic values and human rights are upheld, and to work for international peace and solidarity in an interdependent world.

3. Another and no less fundamental aim of educational development is the transmission and enrichment of common cultural and moral values. It is in these values that the individuals and society find their identity and worth.

4. Basic education is more than an end in itself. It is the foundation for lifelong learning and human development on which countries may build, systematically, further levels and types of education and training.

EDUCATION FOR ALL: AN EXPANDED VISION AND A RENEWED COMMITMENT

ARTICLE 2 ● SHAPING The Vision

1. To serve the basic learning needs of all requires more than a recommitment to basic education as it now exists. What is needed is an "expanded vision" that surpasses present resource levels, institutional structures, curricula, and conventional delivery systems while building on the best in current practices. New possibilities exist today which result from the convergence of the increase in information and the unprecedented capacity to communicate. We must seize them with creativity and determination for increased effectiveness.

2. As elaborated in Articles III-VII, the expanded vision encompasses:

- Universalizing access and prompting equity;
- Focussing on learning;
- Broadening the means and scope of basic education;
- Enhancing the environment for learning;
- Strengthening partnerships.

3. The realization of an enormous potential for human progress and empowerment is contingent upon whether people can be enabled to acquire the education and the start needed to tap into the ever-expanding pool of relevant knowledge and the new means for sharing this knowledge.

ARTICLE 3 ● UNIVERSALIZING ACCESS AND PROMOTING EQUITY

1. Basic education should be provided to all children, youth and adults. To this end, basic education services of quality should be expanded and consistent measures must be taken to reduce disparities.

2. For basic education to be equitable, all children, youth and adults must be given the opportunity to achieve and maintain an acceptable level of learning.

3. The most urgent priority is to ensure access to, and

improve the quality of, education for girls and women, and to remove every obstacle that hampers their active participation. All gender stereotyping in education should be eliminated.

4. An active commitment must be made to removing educational disparities. Underserved groups: the poor; street and working children; rural and remote populations; nomads and migrant workers; indigenous peoples; ethnic, racial and linguistic minorities; refugees; those displaced by war; and people under occupation, should not suffer any discrimination in access to learning opportunities.

5. The learning needs of the disabled demand special attention. Steps need to be taken to provide equal access to education to every category of disabled persons as an integral part of the education system.

Article 4 ● Focussing On Learning

Whether or not expanded educational opportunities will translate into meaningful development—for an individual or for society—depends ultimately on whether people actually learn as a result of those opportunities i.e., whether they incorporate useful knowledge, reasoning ability, skills, and values. The focus of basic education must, therefore, be on actual learning acquisition and outcome, rather than exclusively upon enrolment, continued participation in organized programmes and completion of certification requirements. Active and participatory approaches are particularly valuable in assuring learning acquisition and allowing learners to reach their fullest potential. It is, therefore, necessary to define acceptable levels of learning acquisition for educational programmes and to improve and apply systems of assessing learning achievement.

Article 5 ● Broadening The Means And Scope Of Basic Education

The diversity, complexity, and changing nature of basic learning needs of children, youth and adults

necessitates broadening and constantly redefining the scope of basic education to include the following components:

- *Learning begins at birth*: This calls for early childhood care and initial education. These can be provided through arrangements involving families, communities, or institutional programmes, as appropriate.
- *The main delivery system for the basic education of children outside the family is primary schooling.* Primary education must be universal, ensure that the basic learning needs of all children are satisfied, and take into account the culture, needs and opportunities of the community. Supplementary alternative programmes can help meet the basic learning needs of children with limited or no access to formal schooling, provided that they share the same standards of learning applied to schools, and are adequately supported.
- *The basic learning needs of youth and adults are diverse and should be met through a variety of delivery systems.* Literacy programmes are indispensable because literacy is a necessary skill in itself and the foundation of other life skills. Literacy in the mother-tongue strengthens cultural identity and heritage. Other needs can be served by : skills training, apprenticeships, and formal and nonformal education programmes in health, nutrition, population, agricultural techniques, the environment, science, technology, family life, including fertility awareness, and other societal issues.
- *All available instruments and channels of information, communications, and social action could be used to help convey essential knowledge and inform and educate people on social issues.* In addition to the traditional means, libraries, television, radio and other media can be mobilized to realize their potential

towards meeting basic education needs of all.

These components should constitute an integrated system - complementary, mutually reinforcing, and of comparable standards, and they should contribute to creating and developing possibilities for lifelong learning.

ARTICLE 6 • Enhancing THE Environment FOR LEARNING

Learning does not take place in isolation. Societies, therefore, must ensure that all learners receive the nutrition, health care, and general physical and emotional support they need in order to participate actively in and benefit from their education. Knowledge and skills that will enhance the learning environment of children should be integrated into community learning programmes for adults. The education of children and their parents or other caretakers is mutually supportive and this interaction should be used to create, for all, a learning environment of vibrancy and warmth.

ARTICLE 7 • STRENGTHENING PARTNERSHIPS

National, regional, and local educational authorities have a unique obligation to provide basic education for all, but they cannot be expected to supply every human, financial or organizational requirement for this task. New and revitalized partnerships at all levels will be necessary : partnerships among all sub-sectors and forms of education, recognizing the special role of teachers and that of administrators and other educational personnel; partnerships between education and other government departments, including planning, finance, labour, communications, and other social sectors; partnerships between government and non-government organizations, the private sector, local communities, religious groups, and families. The recognition of the vital role of both families and teachers is particularly important. In this context, the terms and conditions of service of teachers and their status, which constitute a determining factor in the implementation of education for all, must be urgently improved in all countries in line with the joint ILO/

UNESCO Recommendation Concerning the Status of Teachers (1966). Genuine partnerships contribute to the planning, implementing, managing and evaluating of basic education programmes. When we speak of "an expanded vision and a renewed commitment", partnerships are at the heart of it.

EDUCATION FOR ALL : THE REQUIREMENTS

ARTICLE 8 ● DEVELOPING A SUPPORTIVE POLICY CONTEXT

1. Supportive policies in social, cultural, and economic sectors are required in order to realize the full provision and utilization of basic education for individual and societal improvement. The provision of basic education for all depends on political commitment and political will backed by appropriate fiscal measures and reinforced by educational policy reforms and institutional strengthening. Suitable economic, trade, labour, employment and health policies will enhance learners' incentives and contributions to societal development.

2. Societies should also insure a strong intellectual and scientific environment for basic education. This implies improving higher education and developing scientific research. Close contact with contemporary technological and scientific knowledge should be possible at every level of education.

ARTICLE 9 ● MOBILIZING RESOURCES

1. If the basic learning needs of all are to be met through a much broader scope of action than in the past, it will be essential to mobilize existing and new financial and human resources, public, private and voluntary. All of society has a contribution to make, recognizing that time, energy and funding directed to basic education are perhaps the most profound investment in people and in the future of a country which can be made.

2. Enlarged public-sector support means drawing on the resources of all the government agencies responsible for

human development, through increased absolute and proportional allocations to basic education services with the clear recognition of competing claims on national resources of which education is an important one, but not the only one. Serious attention to improving the efficiency of existing educational resources and programmes will not only produce more, it can also be expected to attract new resources. The urgent task of meeting basic learning needs may require a reallocation between sectors, as, for example, a transfer from military to educational expenditure. Above all, special protection for basic education will be required in countries undergoing structural adjustment and facing severe external debt burdens. Today, more than ever, education must be seen as a fundamental dimension of any social, cultural and economic design.

Article 10 ● Strengthening International Solidarity

1. Meeting basic learning needs constitutes a common and universal human responsibility. It requires international solidarity and equitable and fair economic relations in order to redress existing economic disparities. All nations have valuable knowledge and experiences to share for designing effective educational policies and programmes.

2. Substantial and long term increases in resources for basic education will be needed. The world community, including intergovernmental agencies and institutions, has an urgent responsibility to alleviate the constraints that prevent some countries from achieving the goal of education for all. It will mean the adoption of measures that augment the national budgets of the poorest countries or serve to relieve heavy debt burdens. Creditors and debtors must seek innovative and equitable formulae to resolve these burdens, since the capacity of many developing countries to respond effectively to education and other basic needs will be greatly helped by finding solutions to the debt problem.

3. Basic learning needs of adults and children must be addressed wherever they exist. Least developed and low-income countries have special needs which require priority in international support for basic education in the 1990s.

4. All nations must also work together to resolve conflicts and strife, to end military occupations, and to settle displaced populations, or to facilitate their return to their countries of origin, and ensure that their basic learning needs are met. Only a stable and peaceful environment can create the conditions in which every human being, child and adult alike, may benefit from the goals of this Declaration.

• • •

We, the participants in the World Conference on Education for All, reaffirm the right of all people to education. This is the foundation of our determination, singly and together, to ensure education for all.

We commit ourselves to act cooperatively through our own spheres of responsibility, taking all necessary steps to achieve the goals of education for all. Together we call on governments, concerned organizations and individuals to join in this urgent undertaking.

The basic learning needs of all can and must be met. There can be no more meaningful way to being the International Literacy Year, to move forward the goals of the United Nations Decade of Disabled Persons (1983-92), the World Decade for Cultural Development (1988-97), the Fourth United Nations Development Decade (1991-2000), of the Convention on the Elimination of Discrimination against Women and the Forward Looking Strategies for the Advancement of Women, and of the Convention on the Rights of the Child. There has never been a more propitious time to commit ourselves to providing basic learning opportunities for all the people of the world.

We adopt, therefore, this *World Declaration on Education for All: Meeting Basic Learning Needs* and agree on the *Framework for Action to Meet Basic Learning Needs*, to achieve the goals set forth in this Declaration.

44

Framework for Action to Meet Basic Learning Needs

Guidelines for Implementing the World Declaration on Education for All

Introduction

1. This *Framework for Action to Meet Basic Learning Needs* derives from the *World Declaration on Education for All,* adopted by the World Conference on Education for All, which brought together representatives of governments, international and bilateral development agencies, and non-governmental organizations. Based on the best collective knowledge and the commitment of these partners, the *Framework* is intended as a reference and guide for national governments, international organizations, bilateral aid agencies, non-governmental organizations (NGOs), and all those committed to the goal of Education for All, in formulating their own plans of action for implementing the **World Declaration**. It describes three broad levels of concerted action : (i) direct action within individual countries, (ii) co-operation among groups of countries sharing certain characteristics and concerns, and (iii) multilateral and bilateral co-operation in the world community.

2. Individual countries and groups of countries, as well as international, regional and national organizations, may use

the *Framework* to develop their own specific plans of action and programmes in line with their particular objectives, mandates and constituencies. This indeed has been the case in the ten-year experience of the UNESCO Major Project on Education for Latin America and the Caribbean. Further examples of such related initiatives are the UNESCO Plan of Action for the Eradication of Illiteracy by the Year 2000, adopted by the UNESCO General Conference at its 25th session (1989); the ISESCO Special Programme (1990-2000); the current review by the World Bank of its policy for primary education; and USAID's programme for Advancing Basic Education and Literacy. Insofar as such plans of action, policies and programmes are consistent with this Framework, efforts throughout the world to meet basic learning needs will coverage and facilitate co-operation.

3. While countries have many common concerns in meeting the basic learning needs of their populations, these concerns do, of course, vary in nature and intensity from country to country depending on the actual status of basic education, as well as the cultural and socio-economic context. Globally, by the year 2000, if enrolment rates remain at current levels, there will be more than 160 million children without access to primary schooling simply because of population growth. In much of sub-Saharan Africa and in many low income countries elsewhere, the provision of universal primary education for rapidly growing numbers of children remains a long-term challenge. Despite progress in promoting adult literacy, most of these same countries still have high illiteracy rates, while the numbers of functionally illiterate adults continue to grow and constitute a major social problem in much of Asia and the Arab States, as well as in Europe and North America. Many people are denied equal access on grounds of race, gender, language, disability, ethnic origin, or political convictions. In addition, high drop-out rates and poor learning achievement are commonly recognized problems through out the world. These very general characterization illustrate the need for decisive action on a large scale, with clear goals and targets.

Goals and Targets

4. The **ultimate goal** affirmed by the *World Declaration on Education for All* is to meet the basic learning needs of all children, youth, and adults. The long-term effort to attain that goal can be maintained more effectively if **intermediate goals** are established and progress toward these goals is measured. Appropriate authorities at the national and subnational levels may establish such intermediate goals, taking into account the objectives of the *Declaration* as well as overall national development goals and priorities.

5. Intermediate goals can usefully be formulated as specific targets within national and subnational plans for educational development. Such targets usually (i) specify expected attainments and outcomes in reference to terminal performance specifications within an appropriate time-frame, (ii) specify priority categories (e.g., the poor, the disabled), and (iii) are formulated in terms such that progress toward them can be observed and measured. These targets represent a "floor" (but not a "ceiling") for the continued development of education programmes and services.

6. Time-bound targets convey a sense of urgency and serve as a reference against which indices of implementation and accomplishment can be compared. As societal conditions change, plans and targets can be reviewed and updated. Where basic education efforts must be focussed to meet the needs of specific social groups or population categories, linking targets to such priority categories of learners can help to maintain the attention of planners, practitioners and evaluators on meeting the needs of these learners. Observable and measurable targets assist in the objective evaluation of progress.

7. Targets need not be based solely on current trends and resources. Initial targets can reflect a realistic appraisal of the possibilities presented by the Declaration to mobilize additional human, organizational, and financial capacities within a cooperative commitment to human development.

Countries with low literacy and school enrolment rates, and very limited national resources, will need to make hard choices in establishing national targets within a realistic timeframe.

8. Countries may wish to set their own targets for the 1990s in terms of the following proposed dimensions :

1. Expansion of early childhood care and developmental activities, including family and community interventions, especially for poor, disadvantaged and disabled children;

2. Universal access to, and completion of, primary education (or whatever higher level of education is considered as "basic") by the year 2000;

3. Improvement in learning achievement such that an agreed percentage of an appropriate age cohort (e.g., 80 per cent of 14 years-olds) attains or surpasses a defined level of necessary learning achievement;

4. Reduction of the adult illiterarcy rate (the appropriate age group to be determined in each country) to, say, one-half its 1990 level by the year 2000, with sufficient emphasis on female literacy to significantly reduce the current disparity between male and female illiteracy rates;

5. Expansion of provisions of basic education and training in other essential skills required by youth and adults, with programme effectiveness assessed in terms of behavioral changes and impacts on health, employment and productivity.

6. Increased acquisition by individuals and families of the knowledge, skills and values required for better living and sound and sustainable development, made available through all education channels including the mass media, other forms of modern and traditional communication, and social action, with effectiveness assessed in terms of behavioral change.

9. Levels of performance in the above should be established, when possible. These should be consistent with the focus of basic education both on universalization of access and on learning acquisition, as joint and inseparable concerns. In all cases, the performance targets should include equity by gender. However, setting levels of performance and of the proportions of participants who are expected to reach these levels in specific basic education programmes must be an autonomous task of individual countries.

Principles of Action

10. The first step consists in identifying, preferably through an active participatory process involving groups and the community, the traditional learning systems which exist in the society, and the actual demand for basic education services, whether expressed in terms of formal schooling or non-formal educational programmes. Addressing the basic learning needs of all means. Early childhood care and development opportunities; relevant, quality primary schooling or equivalent out-of-school education for children; and literacy, basic knowledge and life skills training for youth and adults. It also means capitalizing on the use of traditional and modern information media and technologies to educate the public on matters of social concern and to support basic education activities. These complementary components of basic education activities. These complementary components of basic education need to be designed to ensure equitable access, sustained participation, and effective learning achievement. Meeting basic learning needs also involves action to enhance the family and community environments for learning and to correlate basic education and the larger socio-economic context. The complementarity and synergistic effects of related human resources investments in population, health and nutrition should be recognized.

11. Because basic learning needs are complex and diverse, meeting them requires multisectoral strategies and action which are integral to overall development efforts. Many

partners must joint with the education authorities, teachers, and other educational personnel in developing basic education if it is to be seen, once again, as the responsibility of the entire society. This implies the active involvement of a wide range of partners - families, teachers, communities, private enterprises (including those involved in information and communication), government and non-governmental organizations, institutions, etc. — in planning, managing and evaluating the many forms of basic education.

12. Current practices and institutional arrangements for delivering basic education, and the existing mechanisms for co-operation in this regard, should be carefully evaluated before new institutions or mechanisms are created. Rehabilitating dilapidated schools and improving the training and working conditions of teachers and literacy workers, building on existing learning schemes, are likely to bring greater and more immediate returns on investment than attempts to start afresh.

13. Great potential lies in possible joint actions with non governmental organizations on all levels. These autonomous bodies, while advocating independent and critical public views, might play roles in monitoring, research, training and material production for the sake of non-formal and life-long educational processes.

14. The primary purpose of bilateral and multilateral co-operation should appear in a true spirit of partnership — it should not be to transplant familiar models, but to help develop the endogenous capacities of national authorities and their in-country partners to meet basic learning needs effectively. Action and resources should be used to strengthen essential features for basic education services, focussing on managerial and analytical capacities, which can stimulate future developments. International co-operation and funding can be particularly valuable in supporting major reforms or sectoral adjustments, and in helping to develop and test innovative approaches to teaching and management, where new approaches need to

be tried and/or extraordinary levels of expenditure are involved and where knowledge of relevant experience elsewhere can often be useful.

15. International co-operation should give priority to the countries currently least able to meet the basic learning needs of their populations. It should also help countries redress their internal disparities in educational opportunity. Because two-thirds of illiterate adults and out-of-school children are female, wherever such inequities exist, a most urgent priority is to improve access to education for girls and women, and to remove every obstacle that hampers their active participation.

1. Priority Action at National Level

16. Progress in meeting the basic learning needs of all will depend ultimately on the actions taken within individual countries. While regional and international co-operation and financial assistance can support and facilitate such actions, government authorities, communities and their several in-country partners are the key agents for improvement, and national governments have the main responsibility for coordinating the effective use of internal and external resources. Given the diversity of countries' situations, capacities and development plans and goals, this *Framework* can only suggest certain areas that merit priority attention. Each country will determine for itself what specific actions beyond current efforts may be necessary in each of the following areas.

1.1 Assessing Needs and Planning Action

17. To achieve the targets set for itself, each country is encouraged to develop or update comprehensive and long term plans of action (from local to national levels) to meet the learning needs it has defined as "basic". Within the context of existing education-sector and general development plans and strategies, a plan of action for basic education for all will necessarily be multisectoral, to guide

activities in the sectors involved (e.g., education, information, communications/media, labour, agriculture, health). Models of strategic planning, by definition, vary. However, most of them involve constant adjustments among objectives, resources, actions, and constraints. At the national level, objectives are normally couched in broad terms and central government resources are also determined, while actions are taken at the local level. Thus, local plans in the same national setting will naturally differ not only in scope but in content. National and subnational frameworks and local plans should allow for varying conditions and circumstances. These might, therefore specify:

- studies for the evaluation of existing systems (analysis of problems, failures and successes);
- the basic learning needs to be met, including cognitive skills, values, attitudes, as well as subject knowledge;
- the languages to be used in education;
- means to promote the demand for, the broad scale participation in, basic education;
- modalities to mobilize family and local community support;
- targets and specific objectives;
- the required capital and recurrent resources, duly costed, as well as possible measures for cost effectiveness;
- indicators and procedures to be used to monitor progress in reaching the targets;
- priorities for using resources and for developing services and programmes over time.
- the priority groups that require special measures;

- the kinds of expertise required to implement the plan;
- institutional and administrative arrangements needed;
- modalities for ensuring information sharing among formal and other basic education programmes; and
- an implementation strategy and timetable.

1.2 Developing a Supportive Policy Environment

18. A multisectoral plan of action implies adjustment to sectoral policies so that sectors interact in a mutually supportive and beneficial manner in line with the country's overall development goals. Action to meet basic learning needs should be an integral part of a country's national and subnational development strategies, which should reflect the priority given to human development. Legislative and other measures may be needed to promote and facilitate cooperation among the various partners involved. Advocacy and public information about basic education are important in creating a supportive policy environment at national, subnational and local levels.

19. Four specific steps that merit attention are : (i) initiation of national and subnational level activities to create a broad, public recommitment to the goal of education for all; (ii) reduction of inefficiency in the public sector and exploitative practices in the private sector; (iii) provision of improved training for public administrators and of incentives to retain qualified women and men in public service; and (iv) provision of measures to encourage wider participation in the design and implementation of basic education programmes.

1.3 Designing Policies to Improve Basic Education

20. The preconditions for educational quality, equity and efficiency, are set in the early childhood years, making attention to early childhood care and development essential to the achievement of basic education goals. Basic education

must correspond to actual needs, interests, and problems of the participants in the learning process. The relevance of curricula could be enhanced by linking literacy and numeracy skills and scientific concepts with learners' concerns and earlier experiences, for example, nutrition, health, and work. While many needs vary considerably within and among countries, and therefore much of a curriculum should be sensitive to local conditions, there are also many universal needs and shared concerns which should be addressed in education curricula and in educational messages. Issues such as protecting the environment, achieving a balance between population and resources, slowing the spread of AIDS, and preventing drug abuse are everyone's issues.

21. Specific strategies addressed to improve the conditions of schooling may focus on: learners and the learning process, personnel (teachers, administrators, others), curriculum and learning assessment, materials and physical facilities. Such strategies should be conducted in an integrated manner; their design, management, and evaluation should take into account the acquisition of knowledge and problem solving skills as well as the social, cultural, and ethical dimensions of human development. Depending on the outcomes desired, teachers have to be trained accordingly, whilst benefiting from in-service programmes as well as other incentives of opportunity which put a premium on the achievement of these outcomes; curriculum and assessment must reflect a variety of criteria while materials — and conceivably buildings and facilities as well - must be adapted along the same lines. In some countries, the strategy may include ways to improve conditions for teaching and learning such that absenteeism is reduced and learning time increased. In order to meet the educational needs of groups not covered by formal schooling, appropriate strategies are needed for non-formal education. These include, but go far beyond, the aspects described above, and may also give special attention to the need for coordination with other forms of education, to the support of all interested partners, to sustained

financial resources and to full community participation. An example for such an approach applied to literacy can be found in UNESCO's *Plan of Action for the Eradication of Illiteracy by the Year 2000.* Other strategies still may rely on the media to meet the broader education needs of the entire community. Such strategies need to be linked to formal education, non formal education or a combination of both. The use of the communications media holds a tremendous potential to educate the public and a share important information among those who need to know.

22. Expanding access to basic education of satisfactory quality is an effective way to improve equity. Ensuring that girls and women stay involved in basic education activities until they have attained at least the agreed necessary level of learning, can be encouraged through special measures designed, wherever possible, in consultation with them. Similar approaches are necessary to expand learning opportunities for various disadvantaged groups.

23. Efficiency in basic education does not mean providing education at the lowest cost, but rather the most effective use of all resources (human, organizational, and financial) to produce the desired levels of access and of necessary learning achievement. The foregoing considerations of relevance, quality, and equity are not alternatives to efficiency but represent the specific conditions within which efficiency should be attained. For some programmes, efficiency will require more, not fewer, resources. However, if existing resources can be used by more learners or if the same learning targets can be reached at a lower cost per learner, then the capacity of basic education to meet the targets of access and achievement for presently underserved groups can be increased.

1.4 Improving Managerial Analytical and Technological Capacities

24. Many kinds of expertise and skills will be needed to carry out these initiatives. Managerial and supervisory

personnel, as well as planners, school architects, teacher educators, curriculum developers, researchers, analysts, etc., are important for any strategy to improve basic education, but many countries do not provide specialized training to prepare them for their responsibilities; this is especially true in literacy and other out-of-school basic education activities. A broadening of outlook toward basic education will be a crucial prerequisite to the effective co-ordination of efforts among these many participants, and strengthening and developing capacities for planning and management at regional and local levels with a greater sharing of responsibilities will be necessary in many countries. Pre and in-service training programmes for key personnel should be initiated, or strengthened where they do exist. Such training can be particularly useful in introducing administrative reforms and innovative management and supervisory techniques.

25. The technical services and mechanisms to collect, process and analyze data pertaining to basic education can be improved in all countries. This is an urgent task in many countries that have little reliable information and/or research on the basic learning needs of their people and on existing basic education activities. A country's information and knowledge base is vital in preparing and implementing a plan of action. One major implication of the focus on learning acquisition is that systems have to be developed and improved to assess the performance of individual learners and delivery mechanisms. Process and outcome assessment data should serve as the core of a management information system for basic education.

26. The quality and delivery of basic education can be enhanced through the judicious use of instructional technologies. Where such technologies are not now widely used, their introduction will require the selection and/or development of suitable technologies, acquisition of the necessary equipment and operating systems, and the recruitment or training of teachers and other educational personnel to work with them. The definition of a suitable

technology varies by societal characteristics and will change rapidly over the time as new technologies (educational radio and television, computers, and various audio-visual instructional devices) become less expensive and more adaptable to a range of environments. The use of modern technology can also improve the management of basic education. Each country may reexamine periodically its present and potential technologies capacity in relation to its basic educational needs and resources.

1.5 Mobilizing Information and Communication Channels

27. New possibilities are emerging which already show a powerful impact on meeting basic learning needs, and it is clear that the educational potential of these new possibilities has barely been tapped. These new possibilities exist largely as a result of two converging forces, both recent by-products of the general development process. First, the quantity of information available in the world - much of it relevant to survival and basic well-being - is exponentially greater than that available only a few years ago, and the rate of its growth is accelerating. A synergistic effect occurs when important information is coupled with a second modern advance - the new capacity to communicate among the people of the world. The opportunity exists to harness this force and use it positively, consciously, and with design, in order to contribute to meeting defined learning needs.

1.6 Building Partnerships and Mobilizing Resources

28. In Designing the plan of action and creating a supportive policy environment for promoting basic education; maximum use of opportunities should be considered to expand existing collaborations and to bring together new partners: e.g., family and community organizations, non-governmental and other voluntary associations, teachers' unions, other professional groups, employers, the media, political parties, co-operatives, universities, research institutions. Religious bodies, as well as education authorities and other governmental

departments and services (labour, agriculture, health, information, commerce, industry, defence, etc.). The human and organizational resources these domestic partners represent need to be effectively mobilized to play their parts in implementing the plan of action. Partnerships at the community level and at the intermediate and national levels should be encouraged; they can help harmonize activities, utilize resources more effectively, and mobilize additional financial and human resources where necessary.

29. Governments and their partners can analyze the current allocation and use of financial and other resources for education and training in different sectors to determine if additional support for basic education can be obtained by (i) improving efficiency, (ii) mobilizing additional sources of funding within and outside the government budget, and (iii) allocating funds within existing education and training budgets, taking into account efficiency and equity concerns. Countries where the total fiscal support for education is low need to explore the possibility of reallocating some public funds used for other purposes to basic education.

30. Assessing the resources actually or potentially available for basic education and comparing them to the budget estimates underlying the plan of action, can help identify possible inadequacies of resources that may affect the scheduling of planned activities over time or may require choices to be made. Countries that require external assistance to meet the basic learning needs of their people can use the resource assessment and plan of action as a basis for discussions with their international partners and for coordinating external funding.

31. The individual learners themselves constitute a vital human resource that needs to be mobilized. The demand for, and participation in, learning opportunities cannot simply be assumed, but must be actively encouraged. Potential learners need to see that the benefits of basic education activities exceed the costs the participants must bear, such as earnings foregone and reduced time available

for community and household activities and for leisure. Women and girls, especially, may be deterred from taking full advantage of basic education opportunities because of reasons specific to individual cultures. Such barriers to participation may be overcome through the use of incentives and by programmes adapted to the local context and seen by the learners, their families and communities to be "productive activities". Also, learners tend to benefit more from education when they are partners in the instructional process, rather than treated simply as "inputs" or "beneficiaries". Attention to the issues of demand and participation will help assure that the learners' personal capacities are mobilized for education.

32. Family resources, including time and mutual support, are vital for the success of basic education activities. Families can be offered incentives and assistance to ensure that their resources are invested to enable all family members to benefit as fully and equitably as possible from basic education opportunities.

33. The permanent role of teachers as well as of other educational personnel in providing quality basic education needs to be recognized and developed to optimize their contribution. This must entail measures to respect teachers' trade union rights and professional freedoms, and to improve their working conditions and status, notably in respect to their recruitment, initial and in-service training, remuneration and career development possibilities, as well as to allow teachers to fulfil their aspirations, social obligations, and ethical responsibilities.

34. In partnerships with school and community workers, libraries need to become a vital link in providing educational resources for all learners — pre-school through adulthood — in school and non-school setting. There is therefore a need to recognize libraries as invaluable information resources.

35. Community associations, co-operatives, religious bodies,

and other non-governmental organizations also play important roles in supporting and in providing basic education. Their experience, expertise, energy and direct relationships with various constituencies are valuable resources for identifying and meeting basic learning needs. Their active involvement in partnerships for basic education should be promoted through policies and mechanisms that strengthen their capacities and recognize their autonomy.

2. Priority Action at Regional Level

36. Basic learning needs must be met through collaborative action within each country, but there are many forms of co-operation between countries with similar conditions and concerns that could, and do, assist in this endeavour. Regions have already developed plans, such as the Jakarta Plan of Action on Human Resources, adopted by ESCAP in 1988. By exchanging information and experience, pooling expertise, sharing facilities, and undertaking joint activities, several countries, working together, can increase their resource base and lower costs to their mutual benefit. Such arrangements are often set up among neighboring countries (sub-regional), among all countries in a major geo-cultural region, or among countries sharing a common language or having cultural and commercial relations. Regional and international organizations of the play an important role in facilitating such co-operation between countries. In the following discussion, all such arrangements are included in the term “regional”. In general, existing regional partnerships will need to be strengthened and provided with the resource necessary for their effective functioning in helping countries meet the basic learning needs of their populations.

2.1 Exchanging Information, Experience and Expertise

37. Various regional mechanisms, both intergovernmental and non governmental, promote co-operation in education and training, health, agricultural development, research and

information, communications, and in other fields relevant to meeting basic learning needs. Such mechanisms can be further developed in response to the evolving needs of their constituents. Among several possible examples are the four regional programmes established through UNESCO in the 1980s to support national efforts to achieve universal primary education and eliminate adult illiteracy:

- Major Project in the Field of Education in Latin America and the Caribbean;
- Regional Programme for the Eradication of Illiteracy in Africa;
- Asia-Pacific Programme of Education for All (APPEAL);
- Regional Programme for the Universalization and Renewal of Primary Education and the Eradication of Illiteracy in the Arab States by the Year 2000 (ARABUPEAL).

38. In addition to the technical and policy consultations organized in connection with these programmes, other existing mechanisms can be used for consulting on policy issues in basic education. The conference of ministers of education organized by UNESCO and by several regional organizations, the regular sessions of the regional commissions of the United Nations, and certain trans-regional conferences organized by the Commonwealth Secretariat, Confemen (standing conference of ministers of education of francophone countries), the Organization of Economic Co-operation and Development (OECD), and the Islamic Educational, Scientific and Cultural Organization (IESCO), could be used for this purpose as needs arise. In addition, numerous conferences and meetings organized by non governmental bodies provide opportunities for professionals to share information and views on technical and policy issues. The conveners of these various conferences and meetings may consider ways of extending participation, where appropriate, to include representatives of other constituencies engaged in meeting basic learning needs.

39. Full advantage should be taken of opportunities to share media messages or programmes that can be exchanged among countries or collaboratively developed, especially where language and cultural similarities extend beyond political boundaries.

2.2 Undertaking Joint Activities

40. There are many possible joint activities among countries in support in national efforts to implement action plans for basic education. Joint activities should be designed to exploit economies of scale and the comparative advantages of participating countries. Six areas where this form of regional collaboration, seems particularly appropriate are : (i) training of key personnel, such as planners, managers, teacher educators, researchers, etc.; (ii) efforts to improve information collection and analysis; (iii) research; (iv) production of educational materials; (v) use of communication media to meet basic learning needs; and (vi) management and use of distance education services. Here, too, there are several existing mechanisms that could be utilized to foster such activities, including UNESCO's International Institute of Educational Planning and its networks of trainees and research as well as IBE's information network and the UNESCO Institute for Education; the five networks for educational innovation operating under UNESCO's auspices; the research and review advisory groups (RRAGs) associated with the International Development Research Centre; the Commonwealth of Learning; the Asian Cultural Center for UNESCO; the participatory network established by the International Council for Adult Education; and the International Association for the Evaluation of Educational Achievement, which links major national research institutions in some 35 countries. Certain multilateral and bilateral development agencies that have accumulated valuable experience in one or more of these areas might be interested in participating in joint activities. The five United Nations regional commissions could provide further support to such regional collaboration, especially by mobilizing

policymakers to take appropriate action.

3. Priority Action at World Level

41. The world community has a well-established record of cooperation in education and development. However, international funding for education stagnated during the early 1980s; at the same time, many countries have been handicapped by growing debt burdens and economic relationships that channel their financial and human resources to wealthier countries. Because concern about the issues in basic education is shared by industrialized and developing countries alike, international co-operation can provide valuable support for national efforts and regional actions to implement the expanded vision of basic Education for All. Time, energy, and funding directed to basic education are perhaps the most profound investment in people and in the future of a country which can be made; there is a clear need and strong moral and economic argument for international solidarity to provide technical co-operation and financial assistance to countries that lack the resources to meet the basic learning needs of their populations.

3.1 Cooperation Within the International Context

42. Meeting basic learning needs constitutes a common and universal human responsibility. The prospects for meeting basic learning needs around the world are determined in part by the dynamics of international relations and trade. With the current relaxation of tensions and the decreasing number of armed conflicts, there are now real possibilities to reduce the tremendous waste of military spending and shift those resources into socially useful areas, including basic education. The urgent task of meeting basic learning needs may require such a reallocation between sectors, and the world community and individual governments needs to plan this conversion of resources for peaceful uses with courage and vision, and in a thoughtful and careful manner. Similarly, international measures to reduce or eliminate current imbalances in trade relations

and to reduce debt burdens must be taken to enable many low-income countries to rebuild their own economies, releasing and retaining human and financial resources needed for development and for providing basic education to their populations. Structural adjustment policies should protect appropriate funding levels for education.

3.2 *Enhancing National Capacities*

43. International support should be provided, on request, to countries seeking to develop the national capacities needed for planning and managing basic education programmes and services (see section 1.4). Ultimate responsibility rests within each nation to design and manage its own programmes to meet the learning needs of all its population. International support could include training and institutional development in data collection, analysis and research, technological innovation, and educational methodologies. Management information systems and other modern management methods could also be introduced, with an emphasis on low and middle level managers. There capabilities will be even more in demand to support quality improvements in primary education and to introduce innovative out-of-school programmes. In addition to direct support to countries and institutions, international assistance can also be usefully channelled to support the activities of international, regional and other inter-country structures that organize joint research, training and information exchanges. The latter should be based on, and supported by, existing institutions and programmes, if need be improved and strengthened, rather than on the establishment of new structures. Support will be especially valuable for technical cooperation among developing countries, among whom both circumstances and resources available to respond to circumstances are often similar.

3.3 *Providing Sustained Long-Term Support for National and Regional Actions*

44. Meeting the basic learning needs of all people in all

countries is obviously a long-term undertaking. This Framework provides guidelines for preparing national and subnational plans of action for the development of basic education through a long-term commitment of governments and their national partners to work together to reach the targets and achieve the objectives they set for themselves. International agencies and institutions, many of which are sponsors, co-sponsors, and associate sponsors of the World Conference on Education for All, should actively seek to play together and sustain their long-term support for the kinds of national and regional actions outlined in the preceding sections. In particular, the core sponsors of the Education for All initiative (UNDP, UNESCO, UNICEF, World Bank) affirm their commitments to supporting the priority areas for international action presented below and to making appropriate arrangements for meeting the objectives of Education for All, each acting within its mandate, special responsibilities, and decisions of its governing bodies. Giver. that UNESCO is the UN agency with a particular responsibility for education, it will give priority to implementing the *Framework for Action* and to facilitating provision of services needed for reinforced international co-ordination and co-operation.

45. Increased international funding is needed to help the less developed countries implement their own autonomous plans of action in line with the expanded vision of basic Education for All. Genuine partnerships characterized by co-operation and joint long term commitments will accomplish more and provide the basis for a substantial increase in overall funding for this important sub-sector of education. Upon governments' request, multilateral and bilateral agencies should focus on supporting priority actions, particularly at the country level (see section 1), in areas such as the following :

a. *The design or updating of national and subnational multisectoral plans of action* (see section 1.1), which will need to be elaborated very early in the 1990s.

Both financial and technical assistance are needed by many developing countries, particularly in collecting and analyzing data, as well as in organizing domestic consultations.

b. *National efforts and related inter-country co-operation to attain a satisfactory level of quality and relevance in primary education* (cf. sections 1.3 and 2 above). Experiences involving the participation of families, local communities, and non governmental organizations in increasing the relevance and improving the quality of education could profitably be shared among countries.

c. *The provision of universal primary education in the economically poorer countries.* International funding agencies should consider negotiating arrangements to provide long-term support, on a case-by-case basis, to help countries move toward universal primary education according to their timetable. The external agencies should examine current assistance practices in order to find ways cf effectively assisting basic education programmes which do not require capital and technology intensive assistance, but often need longer term budgetary support. In this context, greater attention should be given to criteria for development co-operation in education to include more than mere economic considerations.

d. *Programmes designed to meet the basic learning needs of disadvantaged groups, out-of-school youth, and adults with little or no access to basic learning opportunities.* All partners can share their experience and expertise in designing and implementing innovative measures and activities, and focus their funding for basic education on specific categories and groups (e.g., women, the rural poor, the disabled) to improve significantly the learning opportunities and conditions available for them.

e. *Education programmes for women and girls.* These programme should be designed to eliminate the social and cultural barriers which have discouraged or even excluded women and girls from benefits of regular education programmes, as well as to promote equal opportunities in all aspects of their lives.

f. *Education programmes for refugees.* The programmes run by such organizations as the United Nations High Commission for Refugees (UNHCR) and the United Nations Relief and Works Agency for Palestine (UNRWA) need more substantial and reliable long-term financial support for this recognized international responsibility. Where countries of refuge need international financial and technical assistance to cope with the basic needs of refugees, including their learning needs, the international community can help to share this burden through increased cooperation. The world community will also endeavour to ensure that people under occupation or displaced by war and other calamities continue to have access to basic education programmes that preserve their cultural identity.

g. *Basic education programmes of all kinds in countries with high rates of illiteracy (as in sub-Saharan Africa) and with large illiterate populations (as in South Asia).* Substantial assistance will be needed to reduce significantly the world's large number of illiterate adults.

h. *Capacity building for research and planning and the experimentation of small-scale innovations.* The success of Education for All actions will ultimately be determined by the capacity of each country to design and implement programme that reflect national conditions. A strengthened knowledge base nourished by research findings and the lessons of experiments and innovations as well as the availability of competent educational planners will be essential in this respect.

46. The coordination of external funding for education is an area of shared responsibility at country level, in which host governments need to take the lead to ensure the efficient use of resources in accordance with their priorities. Development funding agencies should explore innovative and more flexible modalities of cooperation in consultation with the governments and institutions with which they work and co-operative in regional initiatives, such as the Task Force of Donors to African Education. Other Forums need to be developed in which funding agencies and developing countries can collaborate in the design of inter-country projects and discuss general issues relating to financial assistance.

3.4 Consultations on Policy Issues

47. Existing channels of communication and forums for consultation among the many partners involved in meeting basic learning needs should be fully utilized in the 1990s to maintain and extend the international consensus underlying this *Framework for Action*. Some channels and forums, such as the biannual International Conference on Education, operate globally, while others focus on particular regions or groups of countries or categories of partners. Insofar as possible, organizers should seek to coordinate these consultations and share results.

48. Moreover in order to maintain and expand the Education for All initiative, the international community will need to make appropriate arrangements, which will ensure co-operation among the interested agencies using the existing mechanisms insofar as possible: (i) to continue advocacy of basic Education for All, building on the momentum generated by the World Conference; (ii) to facilitate sharing information on the progress made in achieving basic education targets set by countries for themselves and on the resources and organizational requirements for successful initiatives; (iii) to encourage new partners to join this global

endeavour; and (iv) to ensure that all partners are fully aware of the importance of maintaining strong support for basic education.

Indicative Phasing of Implementation for the 1990s

49. Each country, in determining its own intermediate goals and targets and in designing its plan of action for achieving them, will, in the process, establish a timetable to harmonize and schedule specific activities. Similarly, regional and international action will need to be scheduled to help countries meet their targets on time. The following general schedule suggests an indicative phasing during the 1990s; of course, certain phases may need to overlap and the dates indicated will need to be adapted to individual country and organizational contexts.

1. Governments and organizations set specific targets and complete or update their plans of action to meet basic learning needs (cf. section 1.1); take measures to create a supportive policy environment (1.2); devise policies to improve the relevance, quality, equity and efficiency of basis education services and programmes (1.3); design the means to adapt information and communication media to meet basic learning needs (1.4) and mobilize resources and establish operational partnerships (1.6). International partners assist countries, through direct support and through regional co-operation, to complete this preparatory stage. (1990-91).

2. Development agencies establish policies and plans for the 1990s, in line with their commitments to sustained, long term support for national and regional actions and increase their financial and technical assistance to basic education accordingly (3.3). All partners strengthen and use relevant existing mechanisms for consultation and co-operation and establish procedures for monitoring

progress at regional and international levels (1990-1993).

3. First stage of implementation of plans of action. national coordinating bodies monitor implementation and propose appropriate adjustments to plans. Regional and international supporting actions are carried out. (1990-1995).

4. Governments and organizations undertake mid-term evaluation of the implementation of their respective plans and adjust them as needed. Governments, organizations and development agenices undertake comprehensive policy reviews at regional and global levels. (1995-1996).

5. Second stage of implementation of plans of action and of supporting action at regional and international levels. Development agencies adjust their plans as necessary and increase their assistance to basic education accordingly. (1996-2000).

6. Governments, organizations and development agencies evaluate achievements and undertake comprehensive policy review at regional and global levels. (2000-2001)

50. There will never be a better time to renew commitment to the inevitable and long-term effort to meet the basic learning needs of all children, youth and adults. This effort will require a much greater and wiser investment of resources in basic education and training than ever before, but benefits will begin accruing immediately and will extend well into the future - where the global challenges of today will be met, in good measure, by the world community's commitment and perseverance in attaining its goal of education for all.

45

Education for All : Achieving the Goal

The Amman Affirmation

Education is empowerment. It is the key to establishing and reinforcing democracy, to development which is both sustainable and humane and to peace founded upon mutual respect and social justice. Indeed, in a world in which creativity and knowledge play an ever greater role, the right to education is nothing less that the right to participate in the life of the modern world.

Aware of the power and potential of education, the international community committed itself at the World Conference on Education for All held in Jomtien, Thailand, in March 1990, to meet the basic learning needs of every individual. In major conferences since Jomtien, the nations of the world have repeatedly endorsed the central importance of basic education in all aspects of the development process: preserving the environment, managing population growth, combating poverty, promoting social development and creating equality between the sexes. We have now met in Amman, Jordan, at the gracious invitation of His Majesty King Hussein Bin Talal, to review progress toward the goals set in Jomtien and, of even greater importance, to find ways of overcoming presisnt problems and confronting new challenges in order to achieve Education for All (EFA).

Gains Achieved

In the six years since the adoption of the World Declaration on Education for All, there has been significant progress in basic education, not all countries nor as much as had been hoped, but progress that is nonetheless real. Primary school enrolment has increased, an estimated fifty million more children are enrolled today than in 1990. The number of out-of-school children, which had grown inexorably for decades, is also beginning to decline. There are today 20 million fewer out-of-school children of primary-school age than at the start of the decade. This progress is the result of concerted efforts by governments and peoples to extend educational opportunities. New partnerships have emerged, new resources have been tapped and new energies and ideas have been devoted to making education for all reality.

Accompanying these quantitative gains has been a growing emphasis on the quality of education. Without educational content relevant to current needs, without preparation in the learning skills and new knowledge required for the future, and without efforts to improve learning achievement, access, may either serve the purpose intended nor provide the benefits expected. Fortunately, serious reflection, more rigorous planning and a spirit of innovation have prepared the ground in many countries for important educational advances in the years ahead.

We acknowledge the forces of progress at work in all parts of the world: the new dynamism with which Africa is struggling, in difficult circumstances, to reverse the negative trends of the last ten years; the valiant efforts of South Asia to bring basic education to hundreds of millions of people; the increasing political support being given to EFA in the Arab States, which is increasingly perceived as the best preparation for meeting the challenges and uncertainties of the future; and the measures taken in other regions of the world to protect, sustain and enhance the gains that have been made since the Jomtien Conference.

Shortfalls

Yet, if the achievements of the last six years give reason for optimism, they provide no room for complacency. Continued progress requires even more forceful and concerted action, based on good information, sound research and careful analysis aimed at achieving clearly specified results.

No point was more stressed in Jomtien than the urgent need to close gender gap in education, both as a matter of simple equity and as the most effective means for responding to demographic pressures and promoting development. Yet, progress towards this goal has been excruciatingly slow; much more must be done.

The expanded vision of basic education espoused in Jomtien has often been reduced to a simple emphasis upon putting more children into school: an essential step, but only one of many measures needed to achieve EFA.

Early childhood care and development, with its enormous potential and distinctive role in promoting the active learning capacities and the overall well-being and development of children, while receiving greatly increased attention, nonetheless remains seriously under-developed and under-supported in many countries.

This lack of support applies as well to out-of-school literacy and education programmes for adolescents and adults. There are some 900 million adult illiterates in the world, nearly two-thirds of them women. In all societies, the best predictor of the learning achievement of children is the education and literacy level of their parents. Investments in adult education and literacy are, thus, investment in the education of entire families.

There has also been a tendency to focus on basic education without recognizing its essential links to secondary and higher education, as well as to teacher training and the development of technical and vocational skills. The World Declaration on Education for all was intended to empower, not to limit - to purpose minimums, but not to set ceilings.

The Road Ahead

As we look to the end of the century and beyond, the leadership in each country must assume the responsibility for accelerating progress towards EFA, setting firm targets and timetables for achieving them.

International agencies and donors must also pay their full role as partners in the EFA movement, matching national efforts with significantly increased international support, improved co-ordination and greater responsiveness to country priorities.

All EFA partners must learn how to mobilize new resources as well as how to use existing resources more effectively. In the quest for EFA, enhanced political will, greater financial and material resources and improved management are all essential.

Emerging Challenges

In the light of the developments of the past six years, it has become essential to re-examine goals and add new areas and means of action to those set forth in the Jomtien vision:

- Given the trend toward more open societies and global economics, we must emphasize the forms of learning and critical thinking that enable individuals to understand changing environments, create new knowledge and shape their own destinies. We must respond to new challenges by promoting learning in all aspects of life, through all the institutions of society, in effect, creating environments in which living is learning.
- Given the growing recognition and reality of multicultural

and diverse societies, we must respond by including local content as well as cross-cultural in basic education and by acknowledge the essential role of the mother tongue for initial instruction.

- Given escalating violence caused by growing ethnic tensions and other sources of conflict, we must respond by ensuring that education reinforces, social cohesion and democratic governance; We must learn how to use education to prevent conflict and, where crises do occur, ensure that education is among the first responses, thereby contributing to hope, stability and the healing of the wounds of conflict.
- Given debt burdens, restrictions on social expenditure and continuing wasteful expenditure on weapons of war, we must respond with measures to reduce debt burdens, including the transformation of liabilities into assets through debt swaps, policies that promote investments in a nation's people and future, and reforms to the international economic system that give poor countries a chance to earn their way in the world.
- Given rapidly growing numbers of youth at risk, often alienated from society and facing unemployment, we must seek ways to make education more responsive, both to the immediate realities facing these youth, as well as to the changing realities of a world in which basic learning skills are ever more important.

Continuing Challenges

Even as we focus our attention on those new realties and challenges, we must persist in our efforts to meet the goals set forth in the World Declaration on Education for All:

- The priority of priorities must continue to be the education of women and girls. Successful approaches and programmes must be identified in order that they may be replicated and expanded. There can be no enduring success in basic education until the gender gap is closed.

- The training, status and motivation of teachers continue to be at the very core of educational concerns. While we must make better and wider use of technology and media, they can complement, but never replace the essential role of the teacher as the organizer of the instructional process and as a guide and example to the young.

- The full vision of EFA, that of a learning society, recognizes the role of parents, families and communities as the child's first teachers. Both learning and teaching begin at birth and continue throughout life, as individuals work, live and communicate ideas and values by word and example.

- EFA can only be achieved through a broad partnership untied by a shared purpose. It is essential to sustain the spirit of partnership and to broaden it to include all elements of society : Parliaments, religious bodies, voluntary and community groups, the business sector, the media and others. EFA was founded on a faith in partnerships and a belief that , in a shrinking world, we are destined to share fully in the successes as well as the setbacks of other peoples and countries. In the quest to achieve EFA, it is essential that we sustain and enhance this spirit of solidarity.

- The efficient and effective use of resources continues to be essential to the progress of EFA. We must seek more efficient management of education systems, make more effective use of partnerships, draw more systematically upon research and experimentation, and to develop reliable information and assessment systems.

- The right to education has been powerfully reaffirmed by the near-universal ratification of the United Nations Convention on the Rights of the Child. Yet, there are still over 100 million children without access to education. We must respond urgently with new approaches and strategies capable of bringing quality education within the reach of all, including the poor, the remote and those with special educational needs. This calls for a comprehensive effort tailored to the needs of specific populations and based upon the best available expertise and technology.

Renewing the Pledge

Six years ago, at Jomtien, the international community agreed upon the necessity and the possibility of achieving Education for All. Today, we, the participants in the Mid-Decade Review of EFA, reflecting on the experience and knowledge gained during the intervening years, reaffirm that necessity and possibility and re-dedicate ourselves to the essential task of bring the benefits of education to all.

(The Amman Affirmation is the result of the Mid-Decade Meeting of the International Consultative Forum on Education For All, 16-19 June 1996, Amman, Jordan)